Best wishes; Vee

June W. Lamb

THE
LEARNING JOURNEY

ABSORBING LIFE'S LESSONS

JUNE W. LAMB, MFT

BALBOA.
PRESS
A DIVISION OF HAY HOUSE

COVER Artwork by Julie Wolf, Design by Tim McGee
PHOTOGRAPHS by Garrett Lamb
Chapter III, Photograph by Neil Baunsgard
Chapter IV, Garrett Lamb, Model
Chapter VI, Heather L. Klaftenegger, Model
Chapter IX, Haley Parrett, Model

Balboa Press books may be ordered through booksellers or by contacting:
Balboa Press
A Division of Hay House
1663 Liberty Drive
Bloomington, IN 47403
www.balboapress.com
1-(877) 407-4847

ISBN: 978-1-4525-3417-6 (sc)
ISBN: 978-1-4525-3436-7 (e)

Library of Congress Control Number: 2011905914

Printed in the United States of America

Balboa Press rev. date: 5/6/2011

DEDICATION

There have been many lessons from my journey through life. With age and insight it has become clear to me that I had parents whose shoulders I could stand on through the windstorms of life and I am extremely grateful to them for what they taught me. I know my children and grandchildren will learn their own lessons on their own journey, and I dedicate this book to all of them. Because of their existence my life has been enriched beyond measure.

To my children: John, Jeff and Jonie; their spouses, Janet, Stacy and David and to my grandchildren, Kristen, Garrett, Emily, Anna, Nick, Lindsay and Kaylan.

ACKNOWLEDGEMENTS

Every story in this book is true, but it has been necessary to change names and places in order to provide privacy. I am eternally grateful to those whose stories were used to illustrate our universally human experience and I acknowledge great privilege in having been a part of those stories. I have chosen to relate clinical cases which illustrate the power of love and psychotherapy and therefore do not include the cases which came before me that did not result in success. It is not usual for a client to continue therapy when they are not ready to make changes or do not find their therapist compatible.

It has taken years of effort to discipline my use of time in order to complete this undertaking and I have received the generous support and encouragement of so many individuals along the way that it is difficult to name them all. However, they know who they are and I extend my gratitude for the time spent in reading, commenting and contributing to my endeavor to put down on paper this record of a life lived.

Special acknowledgement and thanks must go to my grandson, Garrett Lamb. His inspiration and skill for all photography and formatting is greatly appreciated. I could not have done it without you, Garrett.

It is only when we truly know and understand that we have a limited time on earth—and that we have no way of knowing when our time is up—that we will begin to live each day to the fullest, as if it were the only one we had.

Dr. Elisabeth Kubler-Ross

CONTENTS

DEDICATION   v

ACKNOWLEDGEMENTS   vii

INTRODUCTION   xi

Chapter I: The Hardest Lesson Of All   1

Chapter II: Where Is Authority?   17

Chapter III: You Are Mind And Body   33

Chapter IV: You Are Two   42

Chapter V: Do It Now   51

Chapter VI: Love Thyself?   60

Chapter VII: Marriage Is A Laboratory   68

Chapter VIII: White Knight/Fair Maiden   86

Chapter IX: Feelings Are Guides   97

Chapter X: Psychology and Spiritual Truths   112

AFTERWORD   127

Appendix   139
    RULES OF COMMUNICATION   139
    FEELINGS AS GUIDE   143
    OPTIONS FOR ACTION   145

BIBLIOGRAPHY   147

INTRODUCTION

Why are we here? What is life for? Is there a point? These questions come up in discussions during psychotherapy sessions in my office. Although there are many approaches in attempting to answer them, one of the most effective has been to share my visual image of life's purpose as illustrated on the cover of this book. Without the acceptance of our evolutionary journey from animal to human, one could not make sense of the various levels of consciousness we all experience. And yet, we are each on our own step toward that evolution, experiencing our own soul journey. Without the model presented by our many wise teachers that sees higher consciousness as the goal of our present evolution, it would be difficult to accept the challenges of life that push us in that direction. To see the entire human population on the planet moving toward the goal of "highest" or as scripture says "sons of the most high"—each at our own pace, whether it be fast or slow, makes it possible to let go of resistance to variations of consciousness, lack of or growing self awareness, and to keep focused on where we teach and where we are taught.

Many wise teachers have pointed the way to higher consciousness for me. Some of them were Teilhard de Chardin, Jesus of Nazareth, C.G. Jung, Kahlil Gibran, Elisabeth Kubler-Ross, and Harry Rathbun.

Life is a classroom. It can be tedious when you find yourself in classes where the lessons contradict every truth you believe to be a certainty. When I was a young child, my belief system included simple, dependable rules that had been taught by family, church, and school:

If you are good, life (God) repays you.
If you are bad, you are punished by that same God.

Being good meant following simple rules. The rules are put forth by Protestant, Catholic, Buddhist, Islamic, Judaic or Zen teachers. When these rules are received by a child they are generally accepted as "right" and go unquestioned until they fail the believer. The rules outlined by most religions and social systems are similar in the child's perception: obey your parents, don't tell lies, study hard, marry in your religion, have your children baptized, be moral and loyal to your friends. Further, because of your many contributions to family, a religious institution and the community, you are "protected."

When I found that obeying these rules did not support my experience in real life, I first felt betrayed, then angry, and then determined to find the rules or truths that would support a meaningful journey from birth to death. In my search I determined that truths would no longer be based on the teachings of others without testing them against my personal experiences, discoveries and conclusions. I have found many teachers who guided this exploration and have been fortunate to live in a geographical center where most of them could be heard in person.

My training and clinical experience as a psychotherapist for the past twenty-nine years have given me a perspective on my own journey through life that is constantly supported by the stories told by others who have come to my office. It seems clear to me that through our presence and activities we reveal where we are in that climb toward consciousness. Writing this book is an attempt to share my life story, which included many contradictions to my early belief system. It is also an attempt to understand the development of a new belief system as it has unfolded in my own life and in those of my clients. If, in telling my story, I can inspire another person to face their own contradictions between thought, belief and experience and to act on their need to find a new script by which to live, the effort will have been worthwhile. This new script is compatible with new self awareness, present consciousness and creates the strength to meet all of life's challenges. I am inspired daily when helping clients and watching their growth occur. At the age of eighty-five, the privilege of this profession dismisses any thought of retirement.

The contradictions in my childhood beliefs have all been major turning points in developing a perspective on life that stands the ongoing test of reality, whether painful or joyful, and confirms the dependability of the absolute law of cause and effect, which is universal. My life has been a journey that included the investigation of the source of beliefs; the discovery that change, growth, and learning never stop; and a deep and abiding wonder at the potential of human beings to transcend, transform, and conquer the most painful and terrifying circumstances of life. At some point in our evolution of consciousness I believe we will not need the jarring, fragmenting events we now experience in order to become conscious; we will willingly continue our growth, be it with pain or pleasure.

The first forty years of my life were propelled by traumatic events which required constant attention to strategizing responses. The shock of wartime death when my fiancé was killed in the Battle of the Bulge, and later the puzzling burden of living with a husband who had suffered a lobotomy because of brain cancer, shook and fragmented my understanding of what could be expected in life. However, the strength I found in those experiences made the agonizing wait on a liver transplant list with my second husband many years later more bearable.

After my first husband's surgery and his death seven years later, survival for myself and my three children became the only task I could manage. After all three children had graduated from college, I turned to my longstanding thirst for education. After earning two degrees, a Bachelor's Degree in Interdisciplinary Social Sciences and a Master's Degree in Counseling, I became a licensed psychotherapist at age fifty-six. I was absorbed and elated when studying Freudian, Adlerian, Jungian, and Rogerian theories and the cognitive theory of Albert Ellis which was then controversial.

It was as though a window had opened and gradually I began not only to understand my own life but to realize that most people have similar experiences of confusion and insight as they go through life. I discovered that all humans struggle with resistance, denial, joy, ecstasy, fear, grief, victory and loss. I was moved by the teachings of Elisabeth Kubler-Ross to know that my pain and grief had been given words. Her wisdom not only helped me to finish processing my own challenges but to have a voice for teaching others. In my work I have taught community college classes, trained hospice volunteers, presented weekend seminars and done crisis counseling for high school students. During all this activity I maintained a comfortable income from my private practice. In all of these settings the lessons have come not only from my education but also from my personal life experience in striving for more self awareness and consciousness.

Beginning with a very traditional childhood set in the historical period that experienced the Great Depression, WWII, the advent of high technology (modern automobiles, jets, television, computers, cell phones, the internet) plus the Vietnam and Gulf Wars, and the calamity of 9/11, I have also seen the development of global transportation, the feminist and sexual revolutions, the arrival of the baby boomer generation, radical changes in family life, political chaos, with overwhelming consumerism and technological advances. With all these changes and the more recent advent of world terrorism, no single generation has had to use more energy adapting than people in my age group.

Many times I have found that the wrong question was being asked in attempting to gain stability, understanding, and contentment. Instead of asking when everything would be calm, or when I would have enough material possessions to be happy, what needed to be asked was "What's next?" Although stubbornly determined to find nirvana in this life, I learned that as long as we are walking on this planet, there will continue to be more experiences, more lessons, more victories and more challenges whether we expect it or not. However, too often in my professional work, I have found people believing that their efforts were over after finding the perfect mate, owning a home, creating a family, having the children leave home after completing college, retirement, or some other point in life where they would have a secure hold on happiness and never be challenged again. Pursuing traditional value systems as a means to an *end* frequently ends with the question "Is this all there is?"

The goal of learning to embrace challenge also requires the willingness to experience severe pain. It is helpful to know that in achieving these goals, we gain a new level of wisdom, sensitivity, compassion, and gratitude for life that can bring inner strength, higher consciousness, and peace regardless of outer events. Achievement of these goals can carry one through the impact of the most traumatic internal and external events.

The chapters in this book usually contain two parts. The first is the story of several events in my life that threw me into a sometimes angry pursuit of truth, having felt betrayed by a faulty belief system. However, each event started the necessary process of learning how to survive, understand, and thrive in a constantly changing environment, both inner and outer. From the thousands of lessons I have experienced, I have chosen those which impacted my journey most profoundly and which I have found most helpful in teaching and guiding others. The second part of the chapter is the report of a clinical case in which clients experienced very similar life events.

The constant thrill and privilege of seeing clients respond to counseling has given me a sense of responsibility, not only to pass on hard won insights from my own life, but also to show how many of us meet the same challenges as we constantly struggle to find our way in the complex classroom called "life." My gratitude to my many clients who have opened windows through which I can see and expand my understanding knows no bounds.

There was a time in my life when I felt I could bargain with a higher intelligence to stop pushing so hard if I would promise to keep learning, learning, and learning. The shattering experiences in my life had left me looking everywhere and anywhere for some kind of rock upon which to stand. It was not until I learned to embrace pain as a precursor to growth that I realized I did not want a rock to stand on, but a river in which to flow.

In this book I have summarized how I found my way from traditional religious training to understanding, trust, and an unshakable belief in the dependability of inherent universal law. My discoveries have included a growing knowledge of the interaction of mind and body and a sharpening awareness of the varieties of human response to life's challenges.

Because my own experience included the challenge of my husbands' catastrophic illnesses, I have specialized in working with individuals and their families facing the dilemma of potential death from dangerous illnesses. It is in the midst of such crisis that many of us look at our conditioned view of life that is comfortable at the time and take several steps up in that journey toward consciousness. I have also worked with marriage relationships, family systems, and individuals seeking direction. I have learned that my own inner dialog, identity, and ability to drop resistance to what seemed wrong in my world are key to bringing about inner peace and creative action.

This journey cannot be made without openness to teachers, support, and accepting companions on this extraordinary pursuit of change, adaptation and evolution. I do believe that our children stand on our shoulders, ready to move on in the evolution of consciousness and can take with them some of our insights—not all, but some—in order to avoid having to learn all of life's lessons from the beginning. For whatever it might mean to them, I offer my failures and victories to anyone who is willing to step into the classroom called "life," embracing it as a learning journey.

CHAPTER I

THE HARDEST LESSON OF ALL

The Acceptance of Death

At age nineteen, life seemed predictable. My parents took care of me and taught me how to behave. I was sheltered, clothed, educated and expected to become a responsible adult. Although it was not expected that I would go to college (in my family girls were not encouraged to pursue higher education), marriage and family were nearly guaranteed. But my predictable life did not go according to plan.

In 1941, soldiers going off to the war in Europe were patriots, brave and true. They would come back victorious, be celebrated, and resume that predictable life. The explosion of that simple belief system became my first and hardest lesson in the classroom of life. My high school boyfriend, Doug Jones, didn't come back. He died on a hilltop in Belgium, never to be seen again. The war ended five months after his death and I experienced a chaotic mass of emotions. While wishing to join in celebrating that the war had ended, I carried a dark void of disbelief at the permanence of his death that left me isolated and confused. His was an enormous presence in the class of '43 at Yakima High School. Not only was he President of the class but a star performer in drama and music productions while maintaining an exceptional grade point average in all his class work. It was impossible to imagine such a dynamic, vibrant young man as no longer existing.

It was my first, but not last, lesson in recognizing that there is no escaping the permanence of death and the painful process of grief. My grief was complicated by my need to comfort his family who suffered a myriad of emotions. While they were angry with the German soldier who fired a bullet into their son's head, they also grieved and regretted that they had not helped us marry before he went off to war. In reality, neither of us was ready for marriage, but wartime accelerates the normal drive to enter into committed, lifetime relationships. As my fellow classmates returned from the war front, they joined me in lamenting the loss of a young man so full of talent and promise. Because we had been "steadies" for our junior and senior years, I was inextricably linked in their memories of him and many times they burst into uncontrollable tears when they saw me around town, in a store or visited me at home.

I was surrounded by a pervasive sympathy that both supported and weakened me. Some friends avoided me, not knowing what they could say or not wanting to feel their own pain. Others hesitated to talk of anything other than Doug's death and were taken aback when I laughed or appeared unemotional for even a moment. Thoreau was right when he said "Pity is the brother of contempt." Pity shifted my identity as a strong and intelligent girl to one of "poor June" and left me feeling weak and isolated. The role of "victim" was alien to my experience as a leader and achiever. After a year had passed, exhausted by the confusion of inner and outer disorientation, I fled to another state when the opportunity presented itself.

After settling into a boarding house full of returning veterans, and finding a secretarial job in a law office in downtown San Francisco, I found myself struggling with the desire to reject all of the teachings from my childhood and to live carelessly and rebelliously. I had unwillingly discovered that life could end without preamble and I needed to make the most of my time—an effort tinged with anger and rejection of my former religious beliefs and the discovery of unpredictability.

The "guest house" in San Francisco opened a strange but exciting world to the country girl from Yakima, Washington. These houses were filled as veterans returned from war and resumed their education. Women, no longer needed in munitions factories, sought new employment in big cities. That very first night in the dining room of the boarding house I met Jack and Alex, both of whom had returned from experiences as soldiers on the European battlefront. Both of them were taking advantage of the Veteran's package offered by the U.S. Government for financial assistance in gaining a college education. Both of them needed to augment that assistance by working in the kitchen at the boarding house for additional spending money. Jack was a law student waiting tables and Alex attended mortuary school while employed as an assistant cook. They were roommates and I married both of them, thirty-nine years apart.

Jack and I were married in August, 1949, and were not unlike the thousands of young couples who, making use of GI loans and a burgeoning economy, lived in a brand new home on the San Francisco Peninsula among other couples just like us who were eager to start family life. The entire community was full of hope and promise. Nearly everyone in the neighborhood joined a local church, hosted barbeques and spent hours discussing pregnancies, landscaping and the schedule of the commuter train. Our three beautiful children arrived within four years and were the center of our lives. Soon our schedule was filled with PTA meetings, Cub Scout meetings, choir practice, bridge games and anticipated summer vacations at the beach. After nine years of marriage we had begun to move into a new phase of maturity and satisfaction with our many accomplishments. Once again, life seemed comfortably predictable.

Then one day in July, 1958, my world shattered once again. Jack arrived home from his train commute looking strangely disoriented. He admitted to having a severe headache and immediately went to lie down. His coloring was an unnatural gray with beads of sweat scattered across his forehead. Although the headache passed within half an hour, I wasted no time in making an appointment for him to see our doctor.

3

After a stumbling and flawed process of diagnosis which took six weeks, the doctor called me from his office saying he was rushing Jack to the hospital. The tumor growing in his frontal lobes had finally produced a pressure which could be seen by a simple eye examination. Further tests in the hospital were followed by a rush to operate. Jack's mother flew from Pasadena to join me in the long wait during surgery which went on for eleven hours. My mind refused to entertain the possibility that our idyllic life in suburbia could be at an end or that the children would be fatherless. I spent the hours gulping endless cups of coffee and reassuring his frantic mother that everything was going to be all right.

At last, the neurosurgeon came out of the operating room to tell us that he had removed the frontal lobes of Jack's brain in order to save his life. Cancer had produced a tumor the size of a lemon, which had spread into the mid-brain, where the surgeons dared not go without risking the possibility of total paralysis. The doctor's exhaustion was obvious as he told me: "You will be responsible for him from now on. He will no longer be capable of making decisions or caring for himself. We cannot say how long he will live, but if he recovers from the surgery, the longest we can expect is probably five years." None of this information registered in my exhausted brain and it would be months before I understood the full meaning of the challenge our family faced.

There are many useful strategies and techniques for people facing such adversity to help them monitor the onslaught of emotions and reactions they will experience. I found myself writing as a means to organize my thoughts. The following is an example of my own writing which helped me process my inner turmoil and pain. Writing it out clarified a painful adjustment to a new reality. It had begun when I first noticed my husband's symptoms and I called it:

DENIAL IS A WARM BLANKET

Can't stop to feel, or understand, must complete dinner—can't stop to question or ponder—a birthday to plan for. No time to savor and digest—children to feed—"Cleanliness is Godliness" "Duty is Good."

Why does he look so confused? His day must have been difficult. Something is wrong.

4

More food to prepare—bathrooms to clean.

Is he feeling something he can't talk about? Have I done something to upset him?

Children to bathe—cookies to bake—nothing is wrong.

Why are these headaches so often? Why do I feel so separate? He doesn't seem to feel it.

The dog must be trained—PTA meeting to attend.

Well good. The Dr. knows what is going on. It's only tension. A blackbird keeps flying through my head—"you know something is wrong and it's not tension!"

There is laundry to do—beds to be changed. If you are good and do all your work, you are protected from evil.

Must I dare to contradict the Doctor?—will I be punished? The blackbird keeps flying.

I did it—it's done. I was bossy and aggressive. I said "It's not right, you must listen to me." How daring of me—how nervy to question a doctor. Doctors know what they are doing. Authority is to be listened to.

The blackbird has perched. You can't stop now—you have to be heard. Alone—an alarmist? —a neurotic?

God is good. If you show up in church—baptize your children, nothing bad will happen to you.

Mrs. Lamb, "You could be causing the headaches."

Women must not nag—be bossy—they won't be loved. But I am loved. The doctor has misread me.

More tests? Hospitalization? Grim faces?

There are children to be bathed. The dog must be fed. Life must make sense. Everything will be normal tomorrow.

Mrs. Lamb, your husband must have surgery—
he has a very large brain tumor.

The groceries must be shopped for, the children need new clothes for school. Of course he won't miss the next Cub Pack Meeting. He's their leader.

Mrs. Lamb, your husband's brain tumor was
malignant. We do not expect him to live.

The lawn needs mowing. Is there no reward for virtue? What God? I have done nothing wrong. I cannot be destroyed—my life has always made sense. He's too big to die.

Mrs. Lamb, your husband is suffering major
paralysis—he'll need lots of care. You must be
responsible for him from now on.

"There's no use crying over spilt milk." Don't cry. Don't collapse. You can handle anything—the children need you.

He looks so confused. His head is not his. Where
did he go?

A new reality? Authority <u>must</u> be questioned. They have no answers—just sad faces. None of this is true. It will be different tomorrow. Aloneness is a universal state. Life is cyclical. What cycle is this?

Rules are only perception—there are no dependable rules. God does not have a long arm with which to change anything. Prayer is a joke. Cause and effect are set. God weeps with our pain. Beliefs are imposed. Beliefs can be changed. Are there any answers?

Who took my warm blanket? Where did it go?
It's so cold. Where is everyone?

I see. I must start over—begin again.

My belief system did not include the possibility of a disaster of this magnitude. Having been a "good girl," I expected reward. There seemed no place to go, no place to look for reason. What I had been taught about doctors having answers to anything pertaining to health was not true. The doctors were uncertain. I turned to the religion which had previously gone unquestioned and, taking my hand, the minister looked at me with great sorrow saying, "Have faith." I looked back at him in disbelief and angrily retorted: "I DID."

The man who came home to his children three weeks after surgery was not the man who had left. Changing my perception of his capabilities became a daily task. After hours of sitting still, expressionless and withdrawn, he would suddenly explode in anger, or plunge into the front yard, dressed or not. The children began to alternately fear him and try to take care of him.

In the seven years that followed, before his death, I searched for answers to my questions. Why? How was I to survive and protect his children from the catastrophe that had befallen their father? Did we humans have a right to operate on each other's brain, leaving a shell that appeared to be the person we had loved, but which had rendered them helpless to experience any further normalcy? What God would do this? I had believed God directed all earthly activity and that He was loving and fair. This was not fair. How was I to retain my sanity in a world where our friends commented on the wonderful miracle of his saved life while I lived in a 24-hour nightmare of confusion, anger and fear?

The rules I lived by required an absolute loyalty and protection toward him. When friends and neighbors reveled in how well he looked and how lucky we were, I was able only to nod and attempt a smile. Only the doctors and I knew the full extent of his condition, but when I tried to discuss my quest for understanding with them, I was rebuffed. Their interests were narrowly confined to medical statistics and the physical body. They often commented with surprise at his unusual and steady physical recovery and on my courage in caring for him. They also reminded me that they did not know what direction the remaining tumor might take, and that I might wake up to find him dead at any time. They began cobalt treatments, hoping to delay any further cancer growth in his brain. Eventually it was explained to me that the radiation, while slowing the cancer growth, would also destroy more healthy brain tissue.

They consistently dismissed my belief that events taking place in his life could have a direct effect on his physical health. But as I observed his daily behaviors following the ups and downs in our struggle to survive, I began to understand that the mind and the body were not acting as separate entities as was commonly believed, but were acting in unison.

Jack's partner in business was forced to dissolve their corporation and when we told Jack this news he looked back at us blankly. But within hours, he suddenly began to stumble and to exhibit alarming additional symptoms of mood instability. I rushed him to the doctor's office where I was told that the loss of his business identity and his physical symptoms were not connected in any way. The doctors were puzzled as to the source of his symptoms, but assured me that it had nothing to do with anything happening in his life. Their interests focused on his genetic history or whether he had had a blow on the head when playing football in high school – neither of which held a clue to his illness. Once again we went through tests only to find that there was no medical explanation for his current difficulties.

I looked for other authorities in the world which could offer explanations for the phenomena I observed. I pored over books on brain function, books on spiritual healing, on alternative medicine and psychological tools for survival. Well meaning friends frequently brought materials they felt were relevant to Jack's condition. My anger grew as I realized that no one had the answers I sought.

As our oldest son grew toward becoming a healthy, vital young man, he became the target of Jack's increasing frustrations. These frustrations could spill into unprovoked rage toward our son and end with his father shaking uncontrollably. Once again, I would ask the doctors if these symptoms could be the result of his frustration with his own lost manhood and I was assured, somewhat impatiently, that these behaviors were part of his physical condition and nothing more. Knowing that my son was not old enough to understand his father's condition and was forming impressions of himself and his own value from these experiences, I was desperate to know when this nightmare might end. Our son expressed the belief that his father hated him, and it was with great sorrow that I attempted to help him understand that this was not so. What his father hated was his now limited and blighted ability to live normally, which, though not conscious, was buried deep in his psyche. I was on guard night and day to push away unthinkable thoughts – that we might all be better off if he died.

It is important to remember that what I am relating happened fifty years ago. Since that time there has been an explosion of knowledge concerning the connectedness of the mind and body, the importance of the family system, and a much greater understanding of the function of the brain. The help our family needed in understanding Jack's condition and getting support for our daily struggle was not available at that time. It is because of this family experience and my unsuccessful search for validation in what I was observing that, as a psychotherapist, I have chosen to specialize in working with families where one member is suffering catastrophic illness. The current clinical case included in this chapter is evidence of the great advances that have been made in this field.

Jack lived for seven years after his initial surgery. The first three years were years of adjustment and frustration for me and for our children. Little by little we learned to separate our hopes and expectations from the daily reality of his condition. We learned the profound truth of living life one day at a time. And we learned that detachment doesn't mean you don't care. It means that you do not take as personal responsibility all of the events going on around you and thus save your emotional energy. We learned to be together as a family while roles were oddly topsy-turvy. The children became lookouts for their dad's needs while still enjoying his occasional playfulness. During his fourth year of illness he suffered a return of symptoms that revealed new growth at the old tumor site. Once again, his doctors began aggressive treatment (Jack flatly refused their suggestion of surgery) and he had weeks of linear accelerator radiation. I had already learned that destroying tumor tissue in the brain means destroying brain tissue and so was not shocked when following this second round of radiation, he was even less active and aware. Three years later, after several months of paralysis, he died at the age of forty-three.

Amazingly, having had seven years in which to prepare for Jack's death, I had not organized or created any plan for the family continuing without him. At that time there was no clear direction being taught in the medical world. In spite of the many trials his condition had presented, Jack's absence from our lives created a hole in our hearts which came as a shock, tinged with bitterness. The grief which followed came and went with surprising intensity and depth. At that time Hospice care, which gives guidance after death, did not exist, support groups were unknown, and families relied primarily on other family members and caring friends who had little knowledge of the complicated family dynamics in such a situation.

The hardest lesson in all of life is how to survive loss, how to prepare for loss and how to accept that as long as we are walking on this planet, we will experience loss. I am so grateful that in the succeeding years all of the helping professions have begun to focus on the entire family system, to take care of unfinished business, and to have all of our affairs in order, whether faced with impending death or not.

At the time of this turmoil, my childlike beliefs about where authority existed left me unable to trust my own inner intuitions. Further, I doubted my own authority because I had no college degrees. It never occurred to me to consult my inner voice in my efforts to survive. Because my search for authority was so misdirected, I was continually frustrated and disappointed in what I found. Angrily I withdrew authority from titles, degrees, the medical model and religious institutions. Again, I felt betrayed by my own belief system which I had gradually rebuilt after Doug's wartime death, based mainly on my childhood teachings.

BACK AT THE OFFICE

Comparing the following case history (1999 to 2002) to the experience of my family (1958 to 1965) is like comparing the dark ages to modern life. It is a joy to relate the changes that have taken place.

Polly and Matt were referred to my office by their Oncologist. The fact that this was a referral by a doctor is where our advances begin. The fact is that the medical model now includes many doctors who acknowledge that the emotional state of their patients is an important factor in their ability to deal with treatment and the possibility of healing. This factor often determines whether the patient can maintain a satisfactory quality of life during treatment and be creative if approaching death.

Matt was 35 and Polly was 27. It was obvious in the looks exchanged between them as they sat down that they were very open with each other and frequently exchanged touches as they told their story. In their seven years of marriage they had acquired a lovely home and were both very successful in their work environments. They had agreed from the beginning of their marriage that they did not want children and so had spent hours biking, hiking, and traveling with their many friends when not working in their garden or improving their home.

Matt's was a particularly aggressive form of abdominal cancer and he was receiving chemotherapy in an attempt to prepare him for future surgery. The chemotherapy didn't seem to be having the hoped-for effect, and Matt was experiencing unpredictable assaults of severe pain.

In one of our first sessions, Polly expressed her fears at having been instructed as to how she could inject morphine into the port and catheter implanted in Matt's chest. This would only be necessary if his pain became unbearable and it was not possible to get professional help immediately. While expressing this fear, she also expressed relief in knowing that she was included in the ongoing struggle to keep Matt as comfortable as possible.

We discussed the differences in their two families in handling the dangerous state of health being dealt with. Polly's family kept insisting that her anxiety and fears were exaggerated and refused to consider, discuss, or explore plans for surviving her husband's possible death. Matt's family, on the other hand, was openly concerned not only with Matt's dangerous state of health, but with Polly's anxiety and fatigue caused by her constant attendance to his needs. As we explored ways in which Polly might find support and help, they agreed that Matt's Aunt, who had been a surrogate mother to him, was the family member most likely to bring the strength and support that Polly needed. Together they decided to ask her to come for an extended visit.

At that time it was not possible to bring in a team from hospice unless all curative treatment had ceased and all attention was turned toward palliative care with the doctor's declaration that the patient had less than six months to live. That rule has presently been tempered to allow the guidance of a hospice team when the life expectancy is for one year or less and curative treatment is still being administered. It is called "Transition Care."

Matt and Polly were unusual in that both of them were able to face the realities of Matt's disease. I advised that they live with their feet in two tracks instead of just the track that led to cure. One track must include the possibility of death and by putting one foot on that track, they were able to discuss the need to have legal papers in order, to discuss Polly's plans following Matt's death if it occurred, to make decisions about a funeral or memorial celebration, and to root out any unfinished business regarding relationships or finances. By dealing directly with issues on the track that led to death and making decisions, they both relieved their fears and anxieties and were able to turn their attention to the second track, that on which Matt was still alive and there were many pleasures to be enjoyed.

Too many families are afraid to discuss the track that might lead to death thinking that in discussing it they will make it happen. Not so. When worries and anxieties regarding end of life plans are avoided, a great deal of energy is used in suppression. Family members, while entertaining the same fears with no acknowledgement, can become alienated from each other. In suppressing their emotional fluctuations they suppress their own body processes, including the immune system, which help keep them well when under stress. When open communication is achieved (sometimes only with professional help) the family is able to share emotions and ideas, to make plans and to remain free of the fear of upsetting each other. It can also happen that the patients become isolated by trying to maintain a "positive" attitude. They are fearful of upsetting the family or appearing to give up. The patient may repress their true feelings and unfortunately, there has been general acceptance that we can save our lives simply by keeping a positive attitude. **Experiencing a painful reality is the only way through it.**

If all those close to the patient are able to face and express the wide range of emotions being experienced, including their hopes, they retain closeness and are mutually supportive in this difficult time. They are then able to put a foot on the track that leads to life and to make daily plans for enjoying whatever quality of life is possible. Some patients enjoy company and set up a regular schedule for visitors. Others spend hours reminiscing and leafing through family albums and memorabilia. Some patients plan trips to be taken in the future when their health allows or they set up tournaments for favorite card games among family members and friends. There is no such thing as "false hope"—those two words having no relationship—and no one can rule out miracles.

Matt's favorite pastime was gardening and he spent hours sitting in his garden plotting out new beds, and with the help of a fellow gardener actually created both vegetable and flower plots that came to fruition long after his death.

Matt and Polly kept regular counseling appointments so that when Matt's aunt came to their home, they had achieved an open communication in which she gladly joined. With her presence, Polly began returning to her work part time and found respite in leaving behind the critical problems of Matt's illness, if only for short periods. A few weeks later Matt's doctors relayed the need for further surgery. Although he voiced reluctance, Matt decided to follow their advice, not for himself, but for Polly. At this time, he had already outlived the original prognosis of death by a full year.

Four weeks after the surgery Matt began to enjoy an increase in energy, was able to move about and declared his desire to "hug a tree". So off he and Polly went for a weekend at their favorite resort—where they enjoyed a second honeymoon that included love making, sightseeing, and their favorite restaurants.

Matt's respite from pain was short-lived and soon the pain returned with such overwhelming force that they were unable to sleep. After further tests, the doctor found Matt's cancer had spread to his bones and liver.

Although the doctor suggested they enlist the help of a hospice team, Matt was unwilling to accept that death could be approaching. It seemed, in his mind, that accepting hospice help meant he had given up and was resigned to going into the dying process. He covered his fears with a mounting anger at his weakening condition and he became "testy"— lashing out at Polly as she became more and more fatigued. Once again, she was given leave from her job with the promise that it would be there when she could return. Matt turned his anger towards his doctor, declaring that he could do more for the pain if he chose and that his doctor "blew him off" by not returning his daily phone calls.

This is a critical time in the care of a patient for whom the medical model holds no further hope. Doctors make their decision regarding possible time left for living based on data, observation, and their wish to help the patient and family experience the best possible quality of life. So when they suggest the help of hospice and the patient or family members resist this as a death sentence, the doctor frequently acquiesces and continues with curative treatment, knowing that it holds no power over approaching death. This can be an enormous frustration to hospice professionals who know how very much their intervention could help everyone concerned.

It was only with sensitive guidance in our professional counseling sessions that Matt was able to see how badly Polly needed help in caring for him. It was pointed out that enlisting the help of hospice was not a death sentence and that on some occasions a patient gets better with hospice support and is graduated from their care. However, the wise assistance of trained hospice personnel was sorely needed in view of Matt's declining health, and he agreed to get that help for Polly's sake. He also began to ask questions about life after death, and to examine the many theories about where the soul goes after physical death. He especially liked the scientific truth that energy cannot be destroyed, only transformed. Matt expressed a strong desire to know why he had such a deadly cancer and read books from many different points of view. He was unable to find any genetic factor, declaring that his family was long lived, but finally accepted that there was great ignorance in all the fields of science as to the many causes of cancer.

Matt was intensely interested in exactly what was happening inside his body and his doctor cooperated by agreeing to ongoing tests although he confided to Polly that the tests would not reveal anything new or treatable. Following one test Matt was unable to breathe and was rushed to the hospital. Because of Matt's desire to fight and his insistence on ongoing curative treatment, the hospice team was briefly forced to withdraw because of their policy at that time. For no apparent reason, Matt had a week of surprising comfort and pleasurable activities that both he and Polly enjoyed. In the meantime, both of their families enlisted the help of prayer groups and felt strengthened by this activity.

Then, also for no apparent reason, the severe pain returned and a visibly weakened Matt declared that he wanted to investigate new research and clinical trials being conducted in New York. At the same time he began plans for projects dealing with home maintenance. He was only mildly aggravated when he was turned down as an appropriate patient for the New York clinical trials and as his strength declined, he began to ask questions about hastening his death. He made his decision clear by refusing food and liquids.

After another emergency trip to the hospital when severe hiccups obstructed his breathing, Matt declared that he would never make another hospital visit and began using a mantra of "Thy will, not mine," indicating his total acceptance of his impotence in fighting his illness any further. The Hospice team gladly returned with all their skills in pain control and support for the entire family system.

In the meantime, Polly tolerated Matt's swings in mood and decline in energy, growing more and more fatigued. Although she became very thin and developed dark circles under her eyes, she never once stopped hoping for more time. When she was down and felt ready for it all to end, Mike rallied, made her laugh and they struggled on.

Matt's style of living did not change during the death process. When his strength permitted, he continued to create wooden carvings, making gifts of them to his visitors. He refused catheterization and struggled with trips to the bathroom or frantic placements of bedpans. He insisted on doing everything for himself that was possible and he delighted in George Bernard Shaw's prose:

> I want to be thoroughly used up when I die,
> For the harder I work, the more I live.
> I rejoice in life for its own sake.
> Life is no brief candle to me.
> It is a sort of splendid torch which I have got
> hold of for a moment and
> I want to make it burn, as brightly as possible,
> Before handing it on to future generations.

Matt died early one morning surrounded by family, friends and hospice caregivers. As frequently occurs, his death was preceded by a three day coma during which Polly scheduled everyone in the family, as well as close friends, a private time to say goodbye. Each of them was assured that Matt could hear what they wished to say since hearing is the last sense we lose when dying.

The service commemorating Matt's life was held several weeks later at a nearby beach where friends, family and caregivers gathered to barbeque and share memories of his all-too-short life.

Those who feel that the focus of my professional work with catastrophic illness must be a great burden or leave me with great pain and sorrow need only hear such stories as Matt's and Polly's to know that I am continually inspired and awed by the courage of those clients who allow me to accompany them on this part of life's journey. They are my teachers as well.

CHAPTER II

WHERE IS AUTHORITY?

Contrary to what we have assumed, **whether we act as a child or an adult hinges more on the issue of authority than on the age and development of our body.** All of us know men or women biologically developed to the point of middle age who still look to the authority of their parents. Others still give authority to anyone with initials after their name, regardless of their wisdom.

As a child, we need to have safe boundaries set by those in authority, usually our parents, teachers, religious leaders, or significant adults, so that we are free to experiment and test without the danger of becoming lost. Somewhere there is an old saying: "He who is not tethered cannot swing." He or she who is not anchored, free within a limited, structured world, knowing what those limits are, is very often fearful and unable to experiment and discover the uniqueness of his or her own person. They live out their lives needing to be told by others, persons in authority, what to think, feel, and do, not having had a safe place to develop their own inner voice.

When my life was ravaged by Jack's illness, the places where I had given authority to provide me with answers had no answers. I had been taught that if you were a "good patient" you followed a doctor's orders without question. Further, my experience with my father's authority made it difficult for me to question any male authority, let alone one with M.D. after his name. When our minister had taken my hand, looked into my eyes and rhetorically advised me to "have faith" I began to question the authority of the church. My "faith" did not seem to be rewarded in light of the recent events.

No consideration was being given for the family system or the environment in which the patient functioned in 1958. At that time this could result in some very difficult misunderstandings between the doctors and those persons close to the patient. But still, I remained convinced that "doctors know best." Several incidents remain imprinted on my mind that caused me to feel impotent and frustrated in dealing with Jack's medical caretakers. In these incidents I gave authority to male figures only to realize much later that my own inner voice was ignored out of habit, although it represented the greater wisdom for solving the problems facing me and the medical professionals.

The first incident was in the process of diagnosis. Jack made the first visit to the doctor's office by himself. After his visit, I was surprised that there were no tests scheduled and the only intervention in his severe symptoms was a prescription for a muscle relaxant. At the same time I felt relieved and I discounted my own observations and alarm at his appearance during the headaches. I convinced myself that the doctor knew what he was doing. Our marriage had been propelled in its early stages by the arrival of three children in rapid succession, the purchase of a lovely suburban home, and Jack's focus on his budding career in merchandising.

In spite of these pressures, and because of our full agreement upon our short term goals, we seldom quarreled or engaged in alienating behavior towards each other. So it was a great shock to find later that the doctor had projected on me the profile of a nagging, dominating wife when I accompanied Jack to his office in an attempt to find a reason for my husband's alarming headaches.

In my mind I questioned whether Jack had described adequately to the doctor how very peculiar and alarming the headaches were. Had he described how strangely his appearance changed when the headaches came on? His face would turn ashen gray and beads of sweat broke out on his forehead. When I realized that Jack did not witness these alarming changes himself I called the doctor's office and asked for a second appointment. I accompanied him into the examination room. When the doctor came into the room and saw me, he looked back and forth between Jack and me and then asked me to leave, saying, "I don't appreciate a wife who feels she needs to speak for her husband. He's perfectly capable of speaking for himself. Perhaps his headaches are from your nagging."

At that time, I, as most people had been taught, did not question a doctor's instruction and, though astonished, I left the examining room and waited in the outer office. Soon Jack came out saying the doctor thought the best thing for him to do was to go on our vacation. It so happened that we had planned a two week vacation which was to commence the week following his second medical appointment. I banished my apprehension about leaving home with the children when he was experiencing such unusual headaches. The doctor felt that getting a change of scenery would make him feel better. So off we went.

We spent two weeks on Balboa Island swimming and playing with the children, visiting relatives and barbequing at our beach cottage. There was only one incident in that two-week span that caught my attention and renewed my worry about his health. When one of the children stood in his way as he was catching a wave, Jack exploded in anger, cursing and yelling in a manner totally unlike his usual conduct. His flash of rage was over quickly, but it left me worrying and his son in a state of shock and confusion at his father's unusual behavior.

When we arrived back home from our vacation, Jack kept the follow-up appointment the doctor had given him. I did not consider accompanying him after my earlier experience in the office. I was at home cooking dinner when I received a phone call from the doctor.

"Mrs. Lamb, I've sent your husband next door to have his eyes dilated. There is a great deal of pressure in his head. The optic nerve is flattened and he will not be able to drive home. You need to come and get him." I was overwhelmed with a mixture of feelings. Fear: what on earth could cause such a sudden state of alarm? Anger: the doctor's manner was abrupt, harsh and demanding. Relief: the doctor was finally acknowledging that something needed attention. When I arrived at his office, having called a neighbor to stay with the children, the doctor ushered me into a private room and announced, "The ophthalmologist has confirmed the pressure I saw in Jack's head, and so I've arranged to admit him to the hospital first thing in the morning to have an angiogram. If he is not there, I can take no further responsibility for his physical condition." I did not understand his terse declaration or the attitude behind it, but once again I silenced my inner voice and joined him in trying to persuade Jack that he must go to the hospital in the morning.

The contrary and perverse behavior that he was to demonstrate for the next seven years was evident when Jack replied: "No. I'm not going to the hospital on a Saturday. It's the weekend and we have plans. I'll be there on Monday but I won't go tomorrow."

Nothing that I or the doctor could say would change Jack's determination to follow through with his weekend plans. Three days later we discovered from the angiogram that there was a large brain tumor in his frontal lobes and he was scheduled for surgery the next morning. The regrettable lack of communication between the doctor and me, and my previous inability to assert my intuitive sense of danger undoubtedly narrowed Jack's chances of surviving. His cancer was very fast growing and had already been given six additional weeks of growth since his headaches were first experienced.

Presently, my professional work with the families I counsel is to help them become co-case managers and to insist upon having an equal voice in making life and death decisions. I see many doctors going to great lengths to include family members in considering all the options open for treatment. Unfortunately, in 1958 we had not reached that point of cooperation between doctor and family. Even in today's enlightened environment, it can be difficult to teach the family to respect their own inner voice and to encourage them to offer their views. Frequently, it is so much easier to leave all responsibility in the hands of those in "authority." Jack's doctor made incorrect assumptions and treated me in a manner which would be considered unprofessional in today's climate of medical knowledge.

As an aside, it was interesting to find myself in a computer class with that same doctor, thirty years later, when he was well into retirement. When he saw my name on the screen which was being managed by the instructor, I saw him turn around and seek me out. At the break, he came to me, putting his hand on my shoulder and said, "I need to tell you I have felt so sorry for not listening to you when your husband was ill. I've never forgiven myself. Yours was such a young and beautiful family. It's something I've not been able to forget." I assured him that the children and I had survived, that they were all doing well, and he should not continue to carry any guilt. As human beings, we are all fallible. What I did not tell him was that I also had carried a burden of guilt for not having asserted myself by insisting that he hear what I had come to tell him in that examining room. The doctor later died while under the care of a hospice team which I had helped train. Life so often comes full circle.

The second time I had a negative confrontation with the authority of the medical professionals was one year after the brain surgery when Jack began nagging me to be allowed to drive his car. He had been left with a great deal of physical paralysis initially, but after a year of physical therapy, often administered by me on our dining room table, he had regained much of his physical movement. Jack seemed totally unaware of the extensive changes in his brain function and considered himself well. The doctors counseled that I should not inform him of the results of his brain surgery. They cautioned that the remaining tumor tissue could activate at any time, and if it reactivated in the motor area of his brain, he could die very suddenly from cardiac arrest. One doctor asked if I would consider having him institutionalized, but my love and loyalty, plus the success I was having in "keeping up appearances" with family and friends, would not allow me to make that decision. His major enjoyment was eating and relaxing in his easy chair.

Once again, as was a necessary pattern by now, I accompanied him into the neurologist's office for his monthly visit where he complained that he should be allowed to drive his car. The doctor looked at me and then, surprisingly, informed me that the state law allowed Jack to drive one year after surgery on the central nervous system if he had not had any blackouts.

I did not usually discuss his limitations in front of Jack, but I was alarmed that the doctor was giving him permission to drive a car after a lobotomy, and I said, "But what about his judgment? What about his rages? What about his lack of responsivity?"

"Well, don't let your children ride in the car if he is driving." he replied.

"What about the children in the other cars?" I asked incredulously.

"Well, you can't keep him imprisoned at home for the rest of his life. He's retained more of his senses than we ever expected and we have no idea how much longer he will live. He must be compensating with other areas of his brain. According to the Department of Motor Vehicles, he is allowed to drive." I felt unheard and once again felt judged as not being sensitive to my husband's needs.

My heart sank as I determined that I would have to be the one to get the DMV to deny him a license since Jack had already heard the doctor's conclusion. I conferred with others regarding my dilemma but the law was clear and in the end Jack resumed his driving. I limited his time behind the wheel as much as possible with flimsy excuses of why I should drive or jumping into the driver's seat before he could. But there were times when he took the car and left by himself without my knowing. Once again I deferred to the authority of an agency in which I had trust—surely the DMV knew what it was doing. He drove without incident for six years and then in a moment of inattention, suffered an accident which left him totally paralyzed and led to my fourth confrontation with his doctors.

However, before that last devastating chapter in Jack's journey through illness, I had acted out the third failure in my willingness to use my inner authority with doctors. It occurred about four years into the illness when he suddenly began stumbling. Filled with alarm and fear that his brain tumor was reactivating, I rushed him to the doctor, only to be referred to Stanford where a new diagnostic tool, the linear accelerator, had recently been constructed. We were met by three doctors who held sheaves of papers and were clearly excited to see a patient with such an unusual history. They ignored me and invited Jack into their examining room and I sat down in the waiting room, not knowing what to expect. My previous experience in joining my husband in the examining room kept me rooted to my seat, but I wondered if they understood how limited he was in verbal responses and how unaware he was of his general mental condition. Should I knock on the door and ask if I might join them, or obediently wait until I was called? After about twenty minutes one of the doctors emerged from the examining room looking frustrated and addressed me by saying, "Mrs. Lamb, your husband is not very cooperative. We have concluded that he is in need of further surgery and he seems unwilling to consider it as an option. He flatly refused our suggestion in no uncertain terms." I learned later that he had told them to F—off.

A part of me was aghast that they expected any modicum of reasonableness from a man who had lived the last four years in a state of limited brain function and another part of me wanted to burst out laughing. I had heard what they called his "uncertain terms" many times in the past four years and had given up protecting others who might recoil in shock. But unable to contain my emotional turmoil, I burst into tears. The youngest of the three doctors immediately put his arm around my shoulders and led me out to the hallway. There I explained my frustration. How could they ignore me and address this man who had such severe limitations, the basis for which must have been clear in his medical records. Did they not understand that I had been totally responsible for him for the past four years and that I had to be included in any decisions made about his health? That young doctor restored my faith by leading me down to the cafeteria, buying me a cup of coffee and listening carefully as I poured out my exasperation with the medical professionals with whom I had to deal.

By the time we returned to the examining room, the other two doctors had patiently explained to Jack that since he flatly refused surgery the only other alternative was to begin linear accelerator treatments and together we set up our first appointment. He was one of the very first to be given a "brain scan" on Stanford's new equipment. As I watched the gages outlining the odd pictures of his frontal brain, my heart sank.

The daily accelerator treatments continued for many weeks, stunning any existing cancer cells, but also destroying healthy brain cells and furthering the brain damage from the initial surgery. I waited with great apprehension, wondering what changes we might experience in our home life and our attempts to lead a somewhat normal life. There had been no blackouts, and once again I consulted with others, seeking support in taking away Jack's driver's license. I did not have the strength or the courage to assert my gut feeling that he should not drive—everyone counseled that we should follow the law. Who was I to take on that authority?

Three years later, on a street very near our home, Jack caused the serious automobile accident which left him in a state of paralysis. Two of our children witnessed the accident and the scene which followed. My oldest son and I arrived at the scene to see the younger son running circles around the overturned car in which Jack rested on his head. Service vehicles came from every direction as their drivers consulted on how to upright his car and remove him to a waiting ambulance. To this day, the children all report that they do not pass that intersection without thinking of their father's overturned car and the flurry of police and firemen as they extricated him from the car and with sirens wailing, sped him to the hospital emergency room, with me at his side.

After two weeks in an acute care hospital it was clear that there was no hope for improvement in his condition. The doctors felt that the accident might have been the result of further tumor growth into the motor area of his brain, or that the impact had caused the paralysis. They were never able to determine the cause for sure, but it was decided to admit Jack to the neurological ward at a veteran's hospital in Palo Alto. Once again, I accompanied him in the ambulance that drove us to the hospital entrance where he was transferred to a steel gurney and placed in an examination room. I was standing beside him when a doctor beckoned me to follow him to the next room. Two other doctors were seated in the room. I was invited to sit down while they looked over Jack's medical records and considered decisions regarding his care. They began consulting among themselves, occasionally asking me questions. Suddenly from the next room came a plaintive call: "June, June, my back hurts." I rose from my chair and headed for the door. One of the doctors put out his hand and said "No, don't leave. He can wait. We need to ask you some further questions."

"But he's lying on a steel table. Can't we make him more comfortable?"

"He's fine. This won't take much longer."

Obediently, I returned to my seat only to hear the continuing call from the next room. "June, June."

And in that fourth time of opportunity to follow my own instincts, I still gave authority to anyone and everyone in the medical model. I never doubted that they had the patient's best interests at heart. My behavior echoed my childhood training of obedience to my father, or any male authority figure. I have not only changed this paradigm for myself but have become successful in helping family and patients see that they must advocate for the care their family members' needs if it is not forthcoming. Now most doctors willingly listen to their patient's or the family's perspective.

Throughout this seven year experience with Jack's illness, I slowly realized that perhaps my own intuitions, ideas, and opinions were valuable and bore the same weight as others, regardless of their credentials. I slowly acknowledged that I was not limited in wisdom because I had no college degree. I began to use new criteria as to whom I could listen. Although some of my teachers carried traditional credentials, I was more interested in the example of their actions. I needed to know that the message and the messenger were one. Their teaching needed to be validated by my own experience of life or, more simply, make sense in light of what I was experiencing.

Others report that they feel more "human" when they are included in the decision making process and retain a sense of identity as an intelligent, reasonable person. In the newer paradigm where doctors include patient and family and offer choices for treatment, some patients are outraged that they are given choices, feeling that only doctors have the knowledge to make such decisions. It is still difficult to teach the family to respect their inner voice and to encourage them to offer their views. Their ability to do this is heavily influenced by how strongly they were conditioned to listen to authority. Sometimes they continue their childhood parental admonitions to repress their anger which then gets expressed in the wrong places. We can only become emotionally healthy when we stop depending upon others to assure us of our value and identity. If we don't, the price is high. Repressed anger usually results in one or all of the following behaviors:

We are defensive.
We blow up easily.
 OR
We feel lost and uncertain.
We become passive.
We are scapegoats to professionals and loved ones.

Parents, schools, and churches, all sources of authority in childhood, can often discourage exploration of ideas, intuitions, fantasies and imaginings. Deviations from medical and religious institutionalized thinking are a nuisance to the institution and challenge their security. Loyalty to institutional doctrine can result in an adult with a child's script which still looks for guidance from other adults wanting the reassurance of being seen as cooperative or "being right." **It is in childhood that we need the opportunity to discover the results of cause and effect, acts and consequences of our behavior. If the experience of discovering fundamental laws is not ours, then it is imposed from a source outside of us, leading us to believe that authority is an external experience.** Laws regarding physical, mental, and emotional life are clearly outlined in all our major religions. Although we need delineated boundaries and guidance as a child, there must be ample room for exploration, mistakes, victories and discovery within those boundaries.

The best of parents often make the common mistake of spending too much time being the authority and disciplinarian for their children, rather than letting results teach the child. Overly attentive parents can deprive their child of experiencing the results of their negative behavior by flying into a rage, lecturing, punishing, or displaying punitive displeasure. When this dramatic display of emotions is unleashed, the child no longer remembers his or her own behavior but refocuses on the "performance" of the parent and the parent becomes the problem. Often the child is awed by the intense reaction of the parent and concludes that they, the child, have valuable power in causing such a "performance." Thus, the child can transfer blame for any discomfort, or inconvenience they experience from their own behavior to the behavior of the parent, blaming them for the consequences of what was really the child's conduct. When this occurs, the original behavior is forgotten and there is no guilt or remorse or learning for the child other than the decision to avoid the parent's reaction, or to punish the parent by causing their "performance" at will.

The child can go through those most important years of development, not learning about himself or herself, but learning about the parental authority figures and how to manipulate them, or to be cowed by them, or to fight them in a constant battle of survival. Later, this attitude towards authority is evidenced in an ability to blame all authority figures—police, bosses, doctors, professors, politicians–for all hurt and failure, and it leaves that person with a child's undeveloped view of the world as a place that consists of persons who know more and wield power over them in all aspects of life. They literally live as a child in an adult body, constantly struggling to keep their place, guarding against anyone or anything that represents more knowledge or more power than theirs. Their identity becomes focused on the role of victim.

Learning to become an adult can begin with a clearer understanding of the authority issue. As adults, we <u>choose</u> where to place authority. No one has authority over us to whom we do not give that authority. For example, authority figures are usually credentialed by our society in one form or another by degrees, licenses, titles, or roles. Some parents hold on to their "credential" of authority through religious teachings which teach "honor thy father and thy mother." However, there is no scripture which adds "and give them authority over your entire life". Unfortunately, some parents are not honorable or lovable, which presents a dilemma for the young and the adult child. My own experience with an authoritative, non-nurturing father had left me with little confidence in my own perceptions of reality. As an adult, I can also defend his actions by acknowledging that he believed he was doing the best thing for his children and was preparing them to face a hostile world by imposing the lessons learned from his own life experience. He did not allow them to discover and create a belief system based on their own unique journey through life.

As adults we must come to the realization that there are credentialed people who cannot be trusted and who do not know as much as we do. We must no longer give authority to others "blindly." We must look for those to whom we wish to give authority and <u>choose</u> to place authority with them because we trust them and can learn something from them. We observe the results of their wisdom in their own lives and consider the whole person in accepting them as our teacher.

As a child we had no such opportunity to "place" authority because we had no reference other than what society and our parents dictated.

We had no power to direct our own lives. Once again, as a child, in order to feel safe, we needed to believe that those bigger than ourselves were "authorities" and could be trusted. As adults, we can use the perceptions we have gained through experience and knowledge to select those from whom we wish to learn, or to whom we give credence in directing our lives. If we are still living in a child's reality, we automatically give authority to those who display the credentials—which means we always follow our parents' wishes, obey the doctor's orders without question, perform whatever religious activities are demanded by the church or synagogue, and allow politicians to remain in office simply because they are there.

As an adult, I choose to give authority to police, highway patrol officers, fire fighters, and to neighbor's property lines. I choose this because it brings order and safety to me and the society in which I choose to exist. However, I feel free to question doctors, professors, politicians, ministers, priests and rabbis. In my psychotherapy practice, I find one of the most common traits of depressed, anxious people is that of giving authority without question, and feeling subjugated to many authorities that cannot be challenged. This leads to resentment, anger, hopelessness and helplessness – all of which can possibly contribute to physical illness by depressing all of the body processes, including the immune function.

BACK AT THE OFFICE

Ed sat down heavily on the edge of the couch, leaning forward and dropping his hands between his knees. He exuded an air of hopelessness as he carefully looked around the office, finally resting his gaze on me.

"I have leukemia. What right does the damn doctor have to give me a death sentence!!? "

As he spoke his voice began to rise and his face clouded with anger.

Slumping against the cushions, he threw his head back and spoke to the ceiling.

"I was diagnosed only two months ago and now they say they don't think they can cure it. This isn't fair. I have three kids and a wife. We just bought a house and we need both our salaries to keep up the mortgage payments."

Listening to the story of Ed's life made it clear that the mortgage was one of the least important factors in his present dilemma. Ed's father had died when he was only eight years old, leaving him with a grieving mother and older brother. Ed carried guilt regarding his father's death because he had hidden and watched from the closet as medics came to speed his father to the hospital following a heart attack. Irrationally, he felt that he should have accompanied him that night and perhaps saved him from death. Children often find ways of blaming themselves for tragic events such as death or divorce because in their stage of development they see themselves as the center of all life. Egocentricity belongs in this developmental stage, although unfortunately we find it rearing its ugly head throughout later stages of development where it is no longer appropriate.

Ed often heard his mother crying at night. He felt their lives were somehow cursed because he had heard his father crying after his grandmother died in the same house. His older brother soon escaped by joining the military service and left Ed with a growing sense of importance in being the sole comfort for his bereaved mother.

During the time between his father's death and his mother's remarriage, Ed saw his mother go through several relationships where he felt she "sold" herself. She also was harshly criticized by his dead father's family. Time after time, Ed repressed his anger and tried unsuccessfully to make his mother happy. His personal loneliness was put aside and he vowed to give his life to his mother even to the point of dying for her.

After her re-marriage he left home, carrying with him considerable rage from his childhood experiences and an inability to see his mother as a fallible human being. He carried with him the certainty that she was his responsibility and he would be available to rescue her from life's tribulations regardless of his own journey. Eventually Ed married, had three children, and at the time of his diagnosis was a successful salesman for a large company.

In psychological theory, Ed had inappropriately given his mother authority over his life and at the time we met she was going in and out of his daily life, criticizing his wife and children while demanding that she be listened to by him. She was generally exhibiting a sense of entitlement to all of his time and energy.

The diagnosis of leukemia had given Ed a target for all of his repressed rage from childhood and he was refusing his doctor's recommendations for a splenectomy to be followed by chemotherapy.

Weeks of counseling followed and eventually Ed was able to see that his rage could have contributed to the onset of cancer by depressing his immune function. Initially, it was difficult for him to see that his relationship with his mother was toxic in its effect on him and his family, and that perhaps his belief system regarding his responsibility for her needed to be revised to include his responsibility to himself and his present life. He struggled in withdrawing authority from her chronic expectations toward him, but finally was able to acknowledge that her present circumstances were the result of her choices, and not that of his failure to make her happy.

As he began to understand his conditioned beliefs, he saw clearly that changes in this relationship were not only justified but imperative in saving his energy to get well. It was almost with a sense of glee that Ed eventually reported he had confronted his mother, told her that he needed a "time out" from her presence in his life and would not be communicating with her further until he was ready. Her shocked response was to withdraw in angry silence and still let him know indirectly that he had "let her down" as the son she could always count on. She flung scripture, accusations of hard heartedness and his father's fictitious disappointment in him as weapons to gain his obedience, but Ed was determined to do everything he had come to realize was necessary in order to regain his health.

The latest research has confirmed that cancer patients who participate in group or individual therapy when dealing with the emotions which can accompany this life threatening illness, have a longer life expectancy. (See Stanford, Dr. David Spiegel, American Psychiatric Assoc., May, 1989). It is important that this information is not used by the patient or doctor to blame the patient for his/her illness. Very few of us would choose to cause cancer in our bodies. However, it is extremely important that the patient is informed of the methods by which they can participate in their treatment through psychological tools that are well known. Extensive experimentation and research continues in this field.

Ed concentrated on medical treatment and the strong support of his wife and family as they faced his struggle to get well. Ed suffered strong negative side effects from the chemotherapy and had to be hospitalized for the scheduled injections because of the violent nausea they created. This reaction could have been linked to his long held resistance to medical authority. He clearly saw that the nausea began before he reached the hospital for the injection and came more from his resistance to treatment than from the chemicals. As he dealt with his residual rage from childhood and reframed his goals, his willingness to accept help from medical professionals increased. At one point, Ed walked into my office carrying a carefully wrapped brownie which he insisted that I try. The cannabis in the brownie had made his visits to the hospital tolerable and he wanted to share his discovery. It was with some regret that I refused his offer, explaining my professional responsibility and the risk that would be involved by my joining him in his discovery.

While in treatment, Ed and his wife Susan began plans to fulfill a lifetime dream of touring Europe by car and Eurail. When his strength permitted, they visited travel agents and poured over maps that would guide them in a six week adventure throughout Europe. In the meantime Ed spent hours playing catch with his seven-year old son, and discussing math assignments with his ten-year old daughter. He reveled in the musical talent of his third child, as her skill on the flute won her awards and honors in school competition. He was astonished at the lightness of spirit he experienced without the constant struggle to meet his mother's demands.

Several weeks passed without their having any communication. In a brief phone call in which she asked if she and her husband might pay a visit, Ed took the opportunity to test his newly-developed inner authority. He agreed that a visit would be welcome but that his current needs for rest would make it impossible for them to stay at his house. He suggested that they come for dinner on the night of their arrival and then retire to a motel, returning for breakfast the next morning. He was firm in stating that a longer visit was out of the question given his and his family's needs. After hanging up the phone, Ed turned to his wife in astonishment saying, "She said that would be fine."

After eleven long months of treatment, Ed was given the good news that his cancer was in remission. It was only six months later that I received a phone call saying that he was feeling very strong and the family was leaving for that dream trip to Europe. It has now been 10 years since Ed met the challenge of cancer. With his health intact, his children in various levels of higher education and with a satisfying career, he takes great pride in his decision to internalize authority by detaching from his mother's sense of entitlement over his life. He spoke at her funeral two years ago and felt a great deal of comfort in having resolved the relationship on a positive note.

Chapter III

YOU ARE MIND AND BODY

Throughout the 20th Century there have been two models for health. The two sciences, medicine and psychology, have eyed each other with suspicion and a competitive edge that have kept them from working together. The medical science formula for data demanded that truth be "measurable, predictable and repeatable." If there was no research data to support this formula, beliefs were discounted as anecdotal.

While evidence grew that brought psychology and medicine into the same arena in treating illness, the psychological model was unable to fulfill the demand of the medical model in establishing scientific data. When attempting to prove the effect on the physical body from emotional stress, it became clear that measuring, predicting and repeating similar patterns of attitude, emotional response, coping mechanisms, mental perceptions from childhood scripts and behavior were almost impossible to fit into the medical model formula for proving theories through control groups and experimentation.

As a result, many impatient supporters of the mind/body theory began to surface. Among them were Robert Ornstein, PhD; Hans Selye, M.D.; Carl Simonton, M.D.; David Siegal. M.D.; Deepak Chopra, M.D.; Andrew Weil, M.D.; Dean Ornish, M.D.; Bernie Siegel, M.D.; Lawrence LeShan, M.D.; and Marty Rossman, M. D.. At this point, the debate is over. Twenty years ago cancer patients came to my office seeking therapy for the emotional aspect of their illness because they had read books, magazine articles, or been convinced of the emotional/physical connection through their own experience. Now, after much moaning and groaning on the part of the medical model, cancer patients are arriving in my office having been referred by their physician. The research goes on and is extensively reported in Dr. Dean Shrock's book "Doctor's Orders: Go Fishing." Some physicians who have openly fought the inclusion of the mental/emotional connections to illness have gracefully conceded and are helping in the re-education of their peers.

Most of us have heard cultural admonitions all of our lives such as:

> "He's a pain in the neck."
> "This gives me a headache."
> "You'll be the death of me."
> "I have butterflies in my stomach."

One would think it would have been clear long before now that our feelings and body processes are working together 24 hours a day.

Why has this taken so long? Initial attempts to point out that we participate emotionally in our physical health were seen as attempts to blame the patient for the illness. I frequently heard new clients declare: "I have cancer and I know that I caused it." In the usual pattern of progress, the pendulum swung to black and white thinking, not realizing that we had simply uncovered another determining factor in our health profile. No one of sound mind would cause themselves to have cancer or suffer from fibromyalgia, multiple sclerosis, muscular dystrophy or any of the other chronic, debilitating disorders that exist. The truth that illness is **multi-causal** has not changed. But we have arrived at the realization that along with genetics, environment, lifestyle, medical services and social connection, we must include our emotional state and its capacity to affect our physiology. When we are emotionally depressed, our physical processes are depressed.

When we are anxious and tense, our physical body is constricted and forced to put therapeutic measures to work in order to protect body function. When our natural healing processes are not functioning optimally, illness is often the result. We have proof that through self-hypnosis, biofeedback and relaxation/imagery, we can directly affect the function of the immune system, cardiovascular, respiratory and digestive systems.

Not only does the medical model accept that the psychological model is an important factor in determining health, but patients are now able to receive health insurance coverage for psychotherapy relating to their illness. Because prolonged grief is such a strong determinant in allowing illness to occur, the diagnosis of "adjustment disorder" is recognized by insurance companies and allows patients the support to process their pain without blocking their natural healing processes.

Grief can be the result of job loss, changed financial security, failure in relationship, or having too many changes requiring adaptation energy happening in a short period of time. All of those pioneers who helped bring about the marriage of the medical and psychological models use the following basic explanation:

> We have two nervous systems, the central and the autonomic. The central nervous system is dominated by our brain, where thoughts, perceptions, truths, rules and lessons learned from life create feelings regarding everything going on around us. It is as though we have a large and growing library of information in our mind as we grow up. It has always been believed that the autonomic nervous system operates without thought, controlling all the body processes: temperature, digestion, respiratory

function, cardiac function and immune function. However, yogis have known for centuries that they can control the autonomic function through highly disciplined practices of yoga, meditation, and a form of self-hypnosis. They have been able to create one temperature on the palm of their hand while creating another on the back of the same hand. Now, through the technology of biofeedback, we have found that most people can be taught this skill by imagining their hand pressed against a block of ice while the sun beats down on the back of the same hand.

We know now that we are participants in our health profile—not the cause—and not necessarily conscious of how this comes about, but nonetheless, participants. If we are to be conscious participants, we must understand how to acquire the tools that allow us to take part in maintaining good health.

Since our feelings come from our mind, from how we see life and our relationship to everything outside us, it is inherent upon each one of us to know the content of that mind—to accept that it is 100% conditioned by our life experience, and we are the only ones who can change scripts that keep us tense, depressed, or anxious. This endeavor needs to be a part of our daily mental activity. Carl Jung proposed that it was our job to bring together the conscious, subconscious and unconscious minds so that, having been assimilated, they represent a powerful base called reality. Understanding the content of these three levels of consciousness can come about through introspection, dream analysis, psychotherapy, or a period of search through reading self help books. As Wayne Dyer said: "You can't solve a problem with the same mind that created it. Change your mind!" Changing your mind can bring about a period of discomfort and uncertainty. Dropping old beliefs means leaving the familiar and testing new ways of seeing life that might make you feel vulnerable.

For instance, you may have come from a family that taught you, "The world is an unfriendly place in which you can't trust anyone, and you should never expect to get what you want. Then you won't be disappointed." **This script may have been taught by a loving parent whose own life experience created it as truth. Their driving need to protect their children from the painful experiences of their own childhood demands that they pass on their negative script.** However, the child who was taught this negative script was powerless and had little choice but to believe the adults they listened to. As adults, we have the power to reconsider those negative beliefs and discard whatever beliefs are not compatible with our own life experience or create unhealthy emotional baggage. Irrationally, many people find it hard to discover that their parents were wrong and to go about creating a new script by which to live. However, growth cannot occur if we are unwilling to "leave home." Realizing that a huge library of beliefs resides in your mind can help you choose which rusty books to toss out, making room for re-considered concepts that come from adult experience. Sometimes we need a model outside ourselves to learn new behavior. Our childhood beliefs are deeply encoded in our brain. We truly do not know other behaviors. Seeing them in another person and then copying them can re-encode our brain and eventually they become ours.

Our understanding of how emotions play upon the physical body by constricting or expanding the body processes makes it imperative to look at negative emotions such as anger, fear, resentment, jealousy, or guilt as health hazards when they are held onto rather than processed. Woody Allen said "I don't get angry, I get tumors." Getting angry is a normal emotional response, not a sin, but it must be processed and not held onto or repressed. The most important thing required if you are going to be a participant in your own state of health is action. There are three things we can do with feelings. We can repress them, refusing to experience them in any way; we can suppress them, knowing they exist but keeping them inside the body; or we can express them, sending that energy to focus outside the body. The only healthy way to deal with feelings is to EXpress them. Otherwise negative feelings remain as depression which constricts the energy inside the body and allows illness to develop. It is also important to express positive feelings in celebration or victory rather than maintaining a calm affect. This is evident in the lack of success in restraining a football player who has just crossed the goal line.

When a cancer patient is referred for counseling we try to include the entire family, opening up communication and finding appropriate ways to express their fears. The medical model used to focus solely on the patient, but we know now that the environment in which the illness takes place, i.e. the family, is equally important because the entire system is affected. Too often families are following a popular belief that they are supposed to be positive when dealing with catastrophic illness. They try to protect each other, avoiding expressing their true feelings. This only suppresses the feelings and adds to the family alienation and tension.

Another important factor is self esteem, a feeling that we deserve to live, that life has meaning and that we have goals that give life purpose. The therapy office is a safe place to look at the two tracks we live on when faced with cancer. Once we have faced our own mortality, we free up energy that might have been used for suppression and move toward life. Once again, Woody Allen said: "I'm not afraid of death, I just don't want to be there when it happens."

It is wrong to call psychotherapy, meditation, or wholistic approaches alternatives to the medical model. No. They are complementary or adjunctive to good medical science. Life can make you sick. Scott Peck began his wonderful book titled The Road Less Traveled with one sentence. "Life is difficult." If possible, we would all prefer to make this journey without accompanying illness. In this combined model there is no promise of cure, no assumptions of sunny outcomes. There is more importantly the acceptance of the challenge and the willingness to address those factors over which we have power: lifestyle, exercise, diet, emotional well-being, relationship issues, spiritual peace, and good medical science. With the new model of mind/body, we, as individuals, carry a great deal of the responsibility for our health with the obvious exceptions being genetics, environment and unavoidable accidents. Our lifestyles, attitudes, coping mechanisms and identity are all important factors in maintaining health. If we can accept physical, mental, and emotional laws we can make the most of the life we have been given.

BACK AT THE OFFICE

Jeannine and her brother Scott arrived at the office after having cancelled two previous appointments. Both appeared to be in their thirties and I had been told that neither was married. They had been referred by a former client who was very worried about their family dynamics in dealing with their father's illness.

In this first session the hostility between them was obvious. Scott sat as far from his sister as was possible and fastened his gaze on the rug in front of him. Jeannine began by saying, "We have to get this settled because if we don't my father will die." As she spoke she glanced nervously in Scott's direction, but continued presenting the critical state of her father's health while Scott continued to stare at the rug.

"The doctors here have given up on healing his cancer," she continued, "But I have heard of an alternative treatment in Greece that cures all the cancer patients who go there. My mother and I want to take Dad there, but Scott has the Power of Attorney and won't help us with the expense for air tickets and a medical attendant to make the trip. The reason Scott has this control over finance is because Mom never learned to deal with money. Dad was always in charge."

My first response was to question whether Dad wanted to make the trip.

"Oh yes, he definitely wants to go on living, but his energy is declining and we can't put off this last chance any longer," Jeannine replied as she reached for a tissue.

Scott leaned forward and retorted, "Dad only wants to keep Mom happy, but he is suffering so much that he is ready to stop all the medical intervention that tries for a cure. He's afraid that the family will see this as "giving up" and he's right. They aren't paying attention to his wishes. This is another crazy idea and the latest since my sister started consulting a psychic. If Dad had his way they would let him die in peace."

Their opposing views of how their father could be helped aroused my greatest sympathy. I also became concerned that the tensions they were experiencing could affect their health and that of other family members. The anxiety regarding their father's health was palpable and I concluded that the entire family system needed to be addressed. After letting both of them express their emotional dilemma, I suggested that it might be helpful if I could see their father.

Two days later I went to their home and was welcomed by a woman who appeared to be in her late sixties. She nervously dried her hands on the apron she wore as she said that she was glad to see me because she didn't know what to do. I told her that I understood the disagreements they were having and would try to help. She led me to the bedroom where a TV blared a noisy football game. As I approached the bed I realized that the occupant was sound asleep. She gently shook his shoulder and as he opened his eyes it was obvious that he was confused and having difficulty orienting himself to the scene before him.

After turning off the TV, his wife left the room and I settled in an easy chair that was conveniently facing him from only a few feet away. He quickly recalled having been told the purpose of my visit and when I assured him that I was willing to discuss anything on his mind he repeated the belief his son had reported earlier in the week. "I can't bear the pain I am causing my family. I have always been the 'strong one' in the family and they can't understand that I want to 'give up.' I feel I am letting them down. I know I couldn't hold up for a flight to Greece but my daughter and wife think it might save my life."

It was clear that the family was caught up in a belief system that has been very common in our culture. The masculine principal mandates that the male be the one who can "fix" everything and many families are taught to lean on his strength no matter what his condition or his personal needs. Even in his frail condition, this man felt a responsibility to appear strong and active to his wife and daughter. In addition, the inability to accept death as a certain outcome for all of us has been sadly neglected in our erroneous sense of control over our lives. Teaching the family to face the reality of his condition was not as difficult as it might appear. Changing the words with which they each described their hopes and fears helped give them an ability to relax and enjoy what remaining life he could expect.

"Giving up" was changed to "being strong in the face of our physical vulnerability." "Being strong" was explained as having the courage to embrace impending death and the privilege of accompanying their father on this final chapter of life. These simple changes in script, although initially faced with resistance, brought them together and let them take care of unfinished business. The realization that her husband and Jeannine's father might die in days, weeks, or months, was difficult for Jeannine and her mother to accept. It was only with several hours of sympathetic listening, during which they fully expressed their grief that they were able to drop their resistance and see that even he was not immortal, as they had believed.

The entire family spent many hours telling him of their love and their appreciation of having had him as their husband and father. The children became the stronghold for their mother and were able to give respite to her tangible grief as their father declined and slipped into a coma.

Too often such tensions in a family facing the death of one of their members results in a subsequent illness for others in the family. Our minds cannot hold negative, guilt ridden, or angry thoughts without lowering the effectiveness of our immune system. All of us have heard of or experienced a serious illness following a stressful period in our lives. All too frequently the surviving spouse falls ill within a year or so of their partner's death. Retirement is frequently followed by declining health. In this instance, the loss involves identity and a depletion of energy from serious life adjustments. Often, a breakdown in health is preceded by several stressful events occurring simultaneously. Coping mechanisms that have served well for much of a lifetime can collapse in the face of multiple energy drains at the same time. In such crises it is important to be self aware and to put in place the necessary protections of rest, exercise, good nutrition and expression of emotions since the mind and body work together twenty four hours a day.

Scott, Jeannine and their mother were able to make final arrangements and discuss needed attention to legal papers so that when the patriarch of the family died, they were not left with guilt or unfinished tasks. When I attended the beautiful memorial service, it was clear that they were enjoying mutual support in suffering the loss of his presence in their lives.

CHAPTER IV

YOU ARE TWO

THE INSIDE/OUTSIDE SELVES

In childhood I struggled every day with the puzzle of how to gain my father's attention. I worshiped the handsome, charming man who was greatly loved by the entire community. I prided myself on his position as Commander of the American Legion Post because he spoke at all of their picnics and my heart pounded as he was wildly applauded while outlining the activities for the day. I felt proud and important as his daughter, then pushed myself with extraordinary effort to win the sack races, the relays and the pie eating contests in order to uphold my responsibility for family honor. I felt rewarded by his fond smile as he announced the contest winners and cherished his pat on the head as I passed the judges stand, my ribbons held high. I walked away intoxicated, believing that I was finally worthy of his love and approval. Anyone watching the proceedings would have assumed a close and traditional family relationship existed in the Wagner household.

Alas, once we arrived home, he returned to his withdrawn, unapproachable and chronically critical role as family patriarch. My shining expectation of further attention from him was met with severe body language that stated he was not as available to his children inside the home as he had been at the picnic. He was not only detached and stern conversationally, he withdrew from any attempt at physical contact, announcing at one point when I tried to stroke his cheek that I was never to touch his face. He spent the better part of his time at home seated at his desk facing a window and all four of his children learned very early that the space around that desk was off limits for any playful or childish behavior. My father suffered from bleeding ulcers (no longer a mystery to me) and our mother was attentive in teaching the children not to argue with their father, or cause him to be upset in any way, lest we cause an episode of bleeding.

During summer months Dad practiced many evenings with the Legion drum and bugle corps on a lighted school ground two blocks away that was visible from my second story bedroom window. On their practice nights, I would remain crouched in an uncomfortable position by my bedroom window for hours, hoping to glimpse him as he passed on the field, blowing his bugle, or having it carefully tucked under his arm. My vigil was seldom rewarded.

Having been born with a strong will and unlimited energy to pursue my desires, I followed every strategy I could imagine to get him to physically communicate his affection for me or openly take pride in my achievements. I won at sports and was told not to talk about it because it made my younger brother feel bad. I won contests in writing and speaking at school, brought home report cards full of "A's" and was told not to get a big head, or brag about my successes. At the same time, I watched him greet neighbors and business acquaintances with a warmth and magnetism that made them smile and melt in the presence of his acceptance and approval.

The result of these dynamics was a growing anger on my part and many outbursts and complaints that he had no right to criticize since he never voiced any approval. I followed him in the hunting fields, hoping to gain his admiration for my quiet pursuance of and attention to his hunting dog's diligence in flushing out pheasants and quail. My younger brother was considered "sickly", and was often fighting one sort of illness or another. So I tried to be the son my father could be proud of by adopting traits which resulted in my being labeled a "tomboy." Little did I know that this was creating a growing fear on my father's part that I was destined to become unsuitable for the roles assigned to women, and because of my outspokenness, my father and I developed an increasing tension and adversarial tone in our relationship.

It was only after years of experience in adult life and with the help of higher education that I was able to understand what had produced such a puzzling contrast in my father's behavior in the outside world and inside our home. There was no way of knowing what lay behind the two faces of my father during that period of my life, but in my professional work as a psychotherapist I have seen the same phenomenon over and over. I have come to not only understand it, but have been able to help others unravel the paradox of our two confusing and oppositional selves.

We all have an "inside" and an "outside" self. The "inside" self is the result of conditioning within the four walls of home and the intimacy, or lack of it, in family relationships. The "outside" self is the result of conditioning outside that home. That self is created by our interaction at schools, playgrounds, with teachers, sports, coaches, literature we have read, social interactions, and peer group approval, inclusion or exclusion.

Confusion results because there are literally two persons inside each one of us and yet we are perceived to be only the visible person of the moment. The relationship with my father resulted in much hurt, confusion and anger on my part. He was, however, unaware of the two selves I was observing and, in truth, believed he was doing his best for me and my siblings. His outside script was the result of his experience in his small

Wisconsin community where he stood out as a smart, charming and likeable young man.

He was the product of his era of history and believed strongly that his daughters had limits in what roles they could expect to fill. At that time girls were expected to become mothers, nurses, teachers or secretaries. In the 1930's there was a beginning of opportunity for higher education for women. However, my father insisted that his three daughters limit their high school curriculum to include all the typing, shorthand and bookkeeping courses that were offered. This was guided by his belief that he should be responsible for their preparation to lead self-supporting lives, and so it was necessary to exclude any unnecessary classes such as those needed for college preparation. At the same time he encouraged his son to plan for college after graduating from high school.

It took me many years to understand how my father could have such sexist beliefs and be so ill-prepared to nurture his children, especially his three daughters. Briefly, his family experience within the four walls of his childhood home was very different from the dynamics he had experienced in the community as a child. His "inside" self had a hidden, and for the most part, unconscious effect on his life within our family.

In his childhood home he was the youngest of five boys. His mother had embraced him as the son she could keep by her side while all the other men in the family worked twelve hours a day on the family farm. She made it clear that he would be the professional in the family after receiving a college education. As a result he was targeted as a weakling by his older brothers as he focused his energy on his studies. However, his parents both died under unfortunate circumstances when he was 10, at which time his brothers insisted he join them in the farm work. The farm work was in sharp contrast to the activities which had gained him a reputation in the Wisconsin farm community as a brilliant student.

In spite of having to learn manual labor after his parents' deaths, he managed to pursue his studies so that he was placed in a one room school house as the teacher at the age of seventeen. And so, in the "outside" world he was a huge success and was popularly thought of as a boy with a great future, while at home he existed in the sad remnants of what had been a happy family before his parents' and one brother's deaths. The contrast in his two selves took a sharp turn as he labored under his older brothers' orders, seldom gaining their approval or affection, which they had little time for, while maintaining the family farm. Within the four walls of home, he was criticized, and perhaps tolerated by his brothers who had never had the unconditional approval or nurturing attention of their dead mother. Since there were no women in the household, little was learned about male/female relationships.

Because of the tragedy within the household of his youth, it became clear to me as I matured that he had no opportunity to develop skills in interpersonal relationships that would help him interact with warmth, affection, or love for four children. At the same time, he had become highly developed in skills of community activity, personal charm and leadership outside the home. What I had experienced as confusion, disappointment and inadequate nurturing as a child was the result of that same lack in his childhood and a huge void in his conditioned "inside" self for meeting the needs of the family he created as an adult. Having lost the dominant relationship of early childhood, that of his mother, he had steeled himself from further pain and chaos by closing the doors to his emotional, feeling self and continued life as an "outside" person who could safely relate to achievement and leadership, using his many skills, intelligence and charm to succeed outside the home. The difference in the two selves was extreme but not recognizable by anyone living outside the family home.

After his parents' deaths, the outside self survived on the limited amount of approval from teachers in the classroom and inclusion by classmates on the playground. Circumstances required that he give up the need for warmth and intimacy at home. It is truly amazing to know the many mechanisms we human beings can put in place in order to survive the fluctuations of psychological development in childhood. Coming to the realization that the father I experienced in our home was the result of necessary defense mechanisms put in place to survive his own childhood became a turning point in my ability to leave childhood baggage behind. It also helped me to understand the relationship he modeled as a husband. My mother never stopped in her efforts to gain his approval with her many domestic skills. However, as their daughter, I was frustrated by the lack of affection or verbal validation she received in return for those efforts. He simply did not have it to give.

Understanding the reason for this dual nature so readily found in many people has allowed me to not only appreciate my father's incredible skills in surviving the lacks in his childhood, but to forgive his lack of ability to nurture his four children through affection and support. It has also spurred me on in my own growth to examine the paradoxes of the inside/outside self and to integrate the best of both selves so that there is congruity for myself and for those with whom I journey through life. I have looked back with great appreciation at the lessons I learned from my father's "outside" self. Lessons regarding the rewards for hard work, organization and strength in pursuing difficult goals, came directly from the model he demonstrated in the community. At the same time, lessons learned from the more painful experiences in my childhood provided the magnetism which drew me to my first husband. This magnetism was clearly based on my need to choose a husband who extended warmth, refinement, unlimited affection and a relationship which provided a new opportunity for my own pursuit of wholeness.

BACK AT THE OFFICE

The new client who walked through my office door was tall, lean and well dressed in a finely fitted suit with a tastefully chosen shirt and tie. I knew only that Gerald's appointment had been made by his wife, which alerted me to the possibility that he was there under protest. He glanced about the room and then rightfully chose to seat himself on the couch opposite the leather easy chair in which I usually sat.

After recording the needed intake data, which included address, phone number, current medications, former counseling experiences, occupation and living circumstances (in which I was told he lived with his wife and three teenage sons), I asked what brought him to my office. Without hesitation, he stated that his wife was tired of the conflicts between him and his three sons and in desperation had asked if he would see a counselor. It was clear that he wanted help as to how to straighten out his three "disrespectful, unappreciative, irresponsible, rude and negligent" sons.

His delight was apparent as he related that the twenty-three employees under his direction as bank manager loved him dearly. They looked to his management as a positive influence in the operation of the bank and often expressed their appreciation for his benevolence in dealing with them as employees. His face softened as he told me of the open door to his office through which employees often walked to tell him their personal problems and to seek his wise guidance in surviving challenges in their lives.

Then his countenance clouded and his voice changed to one of strain and emotion as he related that he could not understand why things were so different at home. His three sons did not listen to his counsel and seemed to deliberately reject his guidance or attempts to be an effective parent by carrying out his responsibility of preparing them for the outside world. They ignored rules, disobeyed directives, and talked back when he reasonably explained to them that they needed to listen and obey. Worst of all, they had begun to avoid him entirely which left him feeling angry and impotent and was beginning to result in frequent outbursts of anger between him and his wife. She defended their sons, declaring that they did not treat her in the same way they treated their father, but complained to her that their father was mean and uncaring.

When I asked for some specific examples of their conflict with him he became quite animated and described his daily homecoming as a perfect example of their disobedient and rude attitude toward him. He related that he had announced that all bicycles, scooters or any other obstacles left in the driveway at the time of his homecoming would be stored in the garage loft or given away as punishment. He felt justified in explaining that since he had worked all day at the bank, he had a right to pull into the garage upon his return home without having to stop and put their toys aside. The boys had listened to this announcement but continued their careless and inconsiderate behavior, leaving the driveway cluttered and impassable almost daily. Gerald's consternation and honest confusion at the difference in the way he was treated at the bank and at home was clearly becoming more and more intolerable (and I wondered if there were physical symptoms of blood pressure or back aches that might accompany this ongoing stress).

As therapy proceeded, Gerald was relieved to find that there were rational reasons for the differences he experienced in his treatment in the workplace and at home. As he examined the contrasting conditionings of his inside self and his outside self, it was clear that his position as boss at the bank reflected his experiences as a student and as a leading player on the high school basketball team. His learned people skills were a direct result of his summer jobs where he worked with underprivileged children, organizing and encouraging their progress in math and reading by keeping strict rules for behavior which earned their respect because of the relief it brought to their chaotic lives.

Gerald slowly realized that he was bringing those same rules of strict discipline and unquestioned authority into his home and into his parenting style. There was nothing in the conditioning of his inside self from which to model a loving parent or to help him create a family where individuals were allowed to explore their individuality while experiencing unconditional love. His alcoholic father had never accepted any variance from the black and white obedience he demanded of his children. The constant reiteration that a father's word was law and that swift punishment would follow disobedience left no room for affection, validation, or expression of feelings.

As therapy progressed, Gerald realized that the hierarchy of power in the workplace made it easy to be boss, and in that setting he allowed himself to express warmth and concern for his employees. But in the setting of home he reverted to a severe style of tyranny, approaching discipline in much the same manner as his father had in his blur of alcohol.

Our therapy sessions became a delight as Gerald began to make changes and reported back on what was taking place at home. We practiced new responses and behaviors to the irritations he found there such as lowering his voice, eliminating angry threats and having family meetings where acts and consequences were openly discussed and suggestions from his sons were listened to. After such a meeting he would thank the boys for their attention and promise that they would be informed of the new rules and consequences of disobedience after he and their mother had made those decisions. Once the rules and consequences were decided upon, they were posted on the refrigerator, thus eliminating the need for any further threats or lectures. Because they were operating as a unit, his relationship with his wife became closer and more enjoyable. The boys soon found that if they tried to argue and bypass the results of their bad behavior, their words were met with quiet patience, followed by "I understand how you feel—the consequence has not changed." Everyone was amazed at how quickly the boys calmed down and even more surprised at how frequently they initiated conversations with their father.

Gerald's awakening to the two selves operating in his life made it possible for him to bring them together and act from an authentic self that others could count on. His pleasure in finding that his sons could not only be cooperative, but were very desirous of his quiet attention and validation, soon made our sessions unnecessary.

Unfortunately, there are no classes required for parenting, although much is known as to how a family can work cohesively for the short time children are under the roof. If a parent has no effective model from which to work, and many people had poor teachers in their own parents, therapy, self-help books and watching effective parents are readily available ways to change dynamics in unhealthy family relationships. Admitting that our parenting is not working is difficult. We seem to want to hang onto our childhood models even when they were ineffective for us. Familiarity has a strong pull in all our behavior but more crippling is the need to believe our own parents were right and we must not question their authority, even as adults. In the process of seeing our parents as human beings, many clients stop the process by suddenly declaring "but I love my parents." Acknowledging human flaws in another, even our parents, does not exclude love. Unfortunately, a healthy relationship with our parents after we have become adults is a topic not well addressed by traditional religious teachings.

The last time I saw Gerald he reported that he and his wife felt certain enough of their sons' responsible behavior to let them stay with individual families while Mom and Dad spent a weekend away. When they returned from their holiday together, Gerald was genuinely surprised at the warm welcome he received from each of his sons and his therapy sessions ended.

CHAPTER V

Do It Now

One of my most treasured teachers was Dr. Elisabeth Kubler-Ross (1926-2004), whose pioneering work helped change American attitudes toward death and dying. Her work of many decades helped establish the hospice movement in this country and brought about more caring and sensitive treatment of terminally ill patients by the medical community. I had the great privilege of studying under her on several occasions.

In her "Life and Death Transition" workshop, which was presented all over the world, she tried to help her students see how vulnerable we humans are and how much more tragic death can be when we are caught unaware and unprepared.

After listening to a story full of regret for unfinished business (which can be unspoken messages between loved ones, unsigned legal papers or alienated relationships), she would turn to her weeping participants and declare in stentorian tones, "Don't vait until it is too late. Take care of your 'unfinished business.' Do it NOW!! Do it NOW!!"

The urgency in her voice made one stop and asks, "What would be left hanging if I were to die today? Who would be hurt by my lack of attention to my own mortality?" As a therapist I often ask myself why some of us come to the end of our lives without ever having accepted that this can happen. Elisabeth's teachings made it clear that we have a choice to process unfinished business or to die in a state of regret.

In the three day seminar she encouraged each of the seventy-five attendees made up of nurses, doctors, priests, ministers, rabbis and therapists to step forward and tell a personal story of painful regret. After enabling the person in front of her and the gathered students to evoke the depth of their pain, Elisabeth would look around to see who was exhibiting feelings and was emotionally ready to work with their own unresolved issues.

After one such session, she caught my eye where I stood in the back of the room and beckoned for me to come forward. I was not sure I was ready to reveal any deeply felt emotions in front of seventy-five people, so I said, "No, what happened to me was fifteen years ago," hoping this would cause her to move on to another attendee. "Vell!" she answered, "Do you vant to carry it for another fifteen years??" Apparently the tears welling in my eyes had given away my vulnerability and hinted at strong, unresolved emotions.

I moved forward to stand in front of this world-renowned therapist and she began by saying, "Tell us your story." I told of my husband's entrance to the Veteran's Hospital after he was paralyzed by the auto accident. I related the scene when three doctors had drawn me into a consultation room after placing him on a metal examination table and began to question me as they combed through his records. I told her how I allowed the doctors to restrain me from going to my husband's side as he moaned in discomfort in the next room, calling my name. As I spoke to Dr. Kubler-Ross at the workshop, I felt a lump forming in my chest. I breathed deeply to control my voice. When I related my obedience to their instruction while Jack continued to plead for help, I began to feel anger, mostly at my own intimidation in their presence.

As I continued with my story, I forgot the surroundings of the workshop and found myself back at the hospital where it took place. My anger built as I visualized the scene when we returned to the examination room and my heart rate accelerated as I remembered the incredible discomfort and pain in Jack's face as they continued to discuss his condition among themselves but well within his hearing. And now, fifteen years later, I finally put into words my anger at what seemed the cold lack of consideration for his comfort but more particularly the deeply felt guilt I carried because I had not demanded that his pleas be addressed. Elisabeth kept probing by repeating "And then vat happened?" until I felt such an overwhelming rush of rage and guilt that I burst into tears. Her Swiss accent was always commanding.

As she had when working with previous students, she then handed me a section of rubber hose with the instruction to stop talking and to "SCRREAMM!" As I began screaming out my pain, I used the hose to beat the mattress upon which I was kneeling—putting my whole body into battering and screaming until I sat back totally exhausted. What I had been so afraid of feeling took less than four minutes to express. During this time the room remained very, very quiet and many in the classroom broke into tears, revealing their own deeply held emotional burdens. The whole drama only lasted about twenty minutes but for me, it seemed an eternity.

After patiently waiting for my emotions to subside, Dr. Kubler-Ross asked, "And who taught you to be buffaloed by doctors?" The answer to that question came easily as I explained my constant but unfulfilled desire to please my father and how that anxiety had been projected on all male authority. She nodded in agreement and then touched me gently on the shoulder saying, "You must promise me that you vill never be buffaloed again."

I returned to my place in the back of the hall feeling extremely light and giddy with relief. A weight that I had carried for fifteen years had been removed in a twenty minute session with a gifted therapist. When I returned home I told my three children about the session with Elisabeth Kubler-Ross. That Christmas they presented me with a stuffed buffalo that still looks at me from a shelf in my grandchildren's playroom.

BACK AT THE OFFICE

I received a phone call one morning from a young man who sounded very tired, asking if I was the therapist who dealt with loss and grief. I answered in the affirmative and questioned how I could help him. He asked if I had a minute to talk and then related the following story. His mother had died five years ago and the family still grieved her absence. Guidance and nurturing had been an important part of his mother's function, and without her, the family was fragmenting into individual realities of confusion and pain as they tried to care for their father, Mervin, who remained in the family home. Mervin was ill and required lots of help which they were trying to provide, but they never knew whether Mervin's discontent was because of his loss or his own illness. The caller stated that he was at a loss as to how to deal with the maze of hurt feelings that no one was discussing and there was a growing alienation among him, his father, his sister and the grandchildren.

Since his father was unable to drive and all the adults in the family were tied up with work responsibilities, I agreed to make a home call and see what possible intervention could help this family in their suffering.

When I arrived at their lovely home in an upscale neighborhood, I was welcomed by a charming woman who told me she was a hired caregiver and that Mervin, the man of the house, was in the family room. As we passed the kitchen I noted another woman busily washing dishes and was told that she, too, was employed as a caregiver for Mervin. The family room was large but cozy, and Mervin was comfortably seated in a large leather lounge chair, feet up, with an oxygen tube attached to his nose. His piercing blue eyes lit up as I entered the room and his smile assured me that my potential intervention was both expected and welcomed. His snow white hair capped a lively, expressive face, and I sat down in an easy chair facing him a few feet away.

"Tell me what's going on here," I began, and after thanking me for coming, he readily offered the following summary of the family situation:

"My son and daughter haven't been to see me since last Sunday, and I'm lonely. Last Sunday they brought their families for dinner and when I asked to be excused from coming to the dining room, they were upset with me and seemed to think that I was just being arbitrary and attention seeking."

"Were you? Is that the first time you haven't joined them in the dining room?"

"Yes. But I was feeling pretty weak and just didn't feel up to it."

"Did you ask them to bring their plates into the family room and eat with you?"

"No, I didn't want to disrupt their dinner, and I felt like resting."

"Mervin, how sick are you?"

"I am on hospice care and since heart surgery, three months ago, the doctors haven't been able to clear up a lung infection. They've tried everything."

"But if you are on hospice care, that means the doctors have predicted that you have six months or less to live. Does your family know that?"

"I don't know if they were told that but I know I'm ready to die. I just don't want to be alienated from my family and would like to see them and talk to them every day if I could. By the way," he grinned, "my wife's name was June, too."

His beaming smile said there was no doubt that this man was very much alive in his willingness to share and to connect at a feeling level.

"Mervin, are you sure your family understands how sick you are? Have they always seen you as strong and in control? Are they having trouble accepting the role reversal that happens when parents are sick or needy?"

"Well my wife was the strong one. We all depended on her strength, and I've been the softy of the family."

I still lacked a real understanding of why last Sunday's dinner had caused a silence from the family members which included two grandchildren and two great grandchildren. I asked the two caregivers who hovered nearby to come into the room and asked if they were seeing a decline in Mervin's health. My own observation told me that he was very, very frail and his breathing was raspy and labored. Both women assured me that they were seeing a daily worsening in his condition and that he frequently had coughing spells that were difficult to stop. When family was there, they would try to help with the coughing by tapping him on the back and urging him to breathe deeply. The caregivers reported that they found it more helpful to gently massage his back until the coughing ceased.

I asked them what it meant to them that he was receiving hospice care. Immediately one reported that when the doctor told the family he would receive this care, he explained that it could only happen if it was declared that Mervin had six months or less to live. Then the doctor had quickly added that Mervin would undoubtedly be alive at the end of six months and he would re-certify his hospice care for another six months. The doctor felt he needed the assistance of a hospice team since Mervin's wife was no longer living. So it seemed that the family was under the impression that his prognosis included another year of life, if not more.

As a psychotherapist, I know that it is ill-advised to become involved in medical prognosis, or to disagree with the medical professionals involved in a case. However, from my long experience with dying patients, I judged that Mervin did not appear to have a very strong hold on life. I asked him how much weight he had lost and was told nearly thirty pounds. Once again, he declared that he was ready to die, but wanted his family around him.

"Mervin, I think we must get the whole family together and talk this out so you can all be on the same page. Do you think they would agree to a family meeting?"

His eyes brightened and he informed me that they were all coming for dinner that night.

"Well, it might be a little soon to spring this on them. They may need more notice."

"No, (as he reached for the phone) I don't see why we can't do it tonight if you're willing to come back." He tapped in a number and then handed the phone to me saying "Here, talk to my daughter."

It was my first hint that I was dealing with a very cooperative and helpful family when she immediately agreed that a family meeting would be a good thing, and asked me to return at 7p.m...

The caregivers walked me to the door and admitted that they were much relieved knowing that something could be done to help the family get back together. They obviously cared deeply for this man and were concerned that the family did not understand his tenuous hold on life.

Arriving back at my office, I received another phone call from his son and I reported what I had observed. He was surprised at my feeling that time was short. He listened carefully to my views but unfortunately had a schedule that would not permit him to be present that evening. I took extra time and carefully explained that I am not a medical professional and have to be careful not to overstep my field of expertise when dealing with patients who are catastrophically ill. In the back of my head I heard Elisabeth's words, "Promise me that you will never be buffaloed again." So I felt it only fair to give him my honest opinion. He assured me that he would visit his father the next day, which was Saturday, and apologize for his absence the previous week.

I arrived back at Mervin's home promptly at seven and was led back into the family room where his daughter, adult granddaughter and her husband were gathered. Once again, Mervin's eyes lit up and he looked around the room as if to say, "Okay, we're going to get this settled."

After I asked for everyone to speak as to what they wanted from this meeting, Mervin's daughter began by saying that she was trying to meet her father's needs but that it was hard to know what was truly needed and what needs were the result of her mother's absence. Her busy schedule prevented her from making daily calls and she thought the two caregivers hired by the family seemed to be taking very good care of him. She was surprised when I said he was feeling lonely for her company. She also reported that she expected her father would live for many more months.

Once again, I risked reporting to her that I did not feel he had very much time and that because he felt ready to die, death might come sooner than expected.

His thirty year old granddaughter then said with great emotion that she was angry with him because in the past few years, he had a pattern of leaving town two weeks out of the month to visit a woman in the next state. She flushed with tears as she angrily stated, "He could have been spending that time with us."

I felt a wave of emotion myself in observing how very attached to her grandfather she felt and how difficult it was for her to accept his impending death. She went on to say that she despised the woman he saw in the other state because of some past history and couldn't understand why he would spend time with her. After a moment of silence, I responded by telling her that she couldn't understand her grandfather's actions now but might when she was much older—that we never stop needing a partner, especially when we have lived a long life in a fulfilling marriage such as Mervin and June's. I expressed my concern that what time was left for this family should be treasured and because the quantity was uncertain, they should make every effort to have quality time with each other.

Glancing at Mervin, I saw that he was following our conversation closely, and I was very touched when he spoke out. He told his granddaughter that he loved her dearly, that she had always been very special to him and to her grandmother—that they had frequently spoken to each other of their pride in her accomplishments. At this, she wept openly in her husband's embrace. Mervin added that now he wanted to be with all of them more frequently and that he wanted to use what time was left to fully enjoy the wonderful family memories that they shared.

A sense of peace began to fill the room as other expressions of love began to pour from all the family members. They wept as they told him they were sorry that they hadn't understood his needs and began to plan how to keep him company on a daily basis.

It was clear that I was no longer needed. I rose and thanked them all for their openness and told them how much I respected them as a family. I turned to the door but was halted as Mervin called out "No, you don't go without a hug" and I turned to find him with both arms stretched toward me. As I leaned over his frail body to embrace him, I was keenly aware of his delicate physical condition.

His daughter walked me to the door, thanking me and assuring me that they would not stop demonstrating the love they had for him. I left also with the assurance that they would have me back as often as Mervin wanted.

Saturday passed and on Sunday afternoon I received a phone call from Mervin's daughter. "June, I need to tell you that Dad just died. We were all here all day Saturday. We had a wonderful, loving time. This morning his caregiver called and said I should get right over there and when I arrived she met me at the door to say 'your father just died.' She had called me because he was having difficulty breathing, but when she finished the phone call, she returned to the family room to find him dead. June, we cannot tell you how grateful we are that we had a chance to mend our differences and to tell him how much we loved him. We believe that having done that, he felt free to go."

We talked a bit longer, both of us experiencing a sense of wonder at the process of living and dying. After we hung up I sat in stillness for some time, filled with an overwhelming gratitude for the extraordinary privilege of working in a field so profoundly rewarding. I felt the blessing of having studied under such teachers as Elisabeth Kubler-Ross, and I was reminded of Dale Borglum's statement, "The most beautiful people I've been around are people who are almost dead." In this instance, I also saw the beauty of his family as they participated in Mervin's final hours.

Elisabeth was right and her admonition to "do it now" needs to be heeded by the sick and the well. No one has a guarantee that he or she will live another day, and no one needs to die with the burden of unresolved negative feelings or regret. We know how to resolve. We know how to untangle those webs we weave. If we don't have the tools ourselves (and few of us do) we can find those who can teach us to live free of the physical constriction caused by guilt, resentment, anger, fear and sadness. We now know how to free ourselves, to live contented, meaningful lives. We know how to use the tool of forgiveness and how to reframe our understanding of life and death, making true the saying:

**"When the reality of death has been faced,
life takes on new meaning".**

CHAPTER VI

LOVE THYSELF?

In line with the thinking of their historical period, my parents taught their children humility, self-deprecation, and that bragging was a sin. All were taught consistently with admonitions such as, "Don't get a big head," "Don't annoy grownups," "Be grateful for what you have," and "Nobody likes a braggart." Besides never making positive comments about their accomplishments, many parents of that era made it clear that children were expected to be seen and not heard, especially if they were angry or crying. "If you're going to cry, go to your room," and "You are selfish if you need to be the center of attention," so "You shouldn't take up other's valuable time," or "Don't interrupt when others are speaking." "Don't show off." "Be quiet and keep your feelings to yourself" were admonitions that were often used by my parents' generation. It was particularly important to them that their three daughters be modest and non-threatening to the male members of the family. This style of parenting was actually done in the hope that the daughters would not be offensive and would attract husbands when the time was right.

If we did not learn from the admonitions and the criticism we received, we needed only to watch the interplay between our parents to understand the model we were expected to follow. At that time in the evolution of consciousness, women did not openly disagree with their husbands or even enter into discussions about serious topics. For the most part, women had no higher education and so did not think themselves worthy of joining a discussion where males held forth.

So it was a startling moment that day in Sunday school when the First Commandment was presented, exhorting the importance of loving God "as you love yourself." I sat in stunned nine year old silence as this commandment, presented with such enthusiasm by the teacher, actually ended with the presumption that you "loved yourself." How very self-centered and egocentric to say that you should "love God as you loved yourself." Surely that wasn't what it meant. This exhortation to love myself as well as God seemed contrary to all my previous training. It seemed that humility and self effacement did not appear in the First Commandment. I was caught between my two major authorities, my parents and the Bible.

However, the surprising feeling of warmth and safety I felt each Sunday when we closed our class by singing "Jesus Loves Me" was puzzling. It felt new to me. Although I had heard the word "love" used at Valentine's Day and was thoroughly convinced by my lessons that "God is Love," I was puzzled as to what place love had in my own limited experience and how I would know it if I felt it. An explanation of the concept of love never seemed to appear.

Although I found the concept startling, I began a secret inner dialog accepting what was for me a revolutionary idea. For obvious reasons, I thought I needed to distance myself from the rest of the family when I indulged in this inner dialog, so I frequently climbed to the top of our pine tree or sat on the chicken house roof and talked to myself about some real or imagined triumph. I daringly congratulated myself for winning a spelling contest or for hitting a home run. When I came home with the announcement that I had won second place in an all-school extemporaneous speaking contest, although I was only a sophomore contestant in the four year high school, I was met with the admonition, "That doesn't mean you're any better than your brother and sisters."

So I retired to the chicken house roof and reassured myself that if I was to love God, I had to love the fact that I had won the contest. So early on I learned to keep my mouth shut if I felt good about myself and to adopt a false modesty towards any compliments and recognition that might come my way.

At that time, many parents had not experienced open affection or verbalization of love themselves and believed that expressions of love could corrupt or spoil a child if given lavishly. The practice of calling out, "I love you," as family members part, which is commonplace in our current culture, was never heard. I also felt ignorant of the place of lips in the romantic stories I began to read since I had never experienced kissing. I often curled my index finger to form two lips and put my mouth against it to see what a kiss might feel like. It did not give me a clue as to why kissing was so important in expressing love. But "love myself?"

It is astonishing to me, in this age of psychological sophistication, that many children are still being given the message that their feelings are unimportant, and that it is impolite to celebrate accomplishment. They are still being taught that they owe a great debt to their parents, that they must hide their successes, that they should be embarrassed when complimented, and that what they have to say is unimportant. Among these people, there is no model for feeling good about accomplishments or being celebrated by others. This style of parenting can leave a deep indelible scar on the child's self esteem that is carried into adulthood.

BACK AT THE OFFICE

When Sophie came to my office, she presented a marital issue with her husband of two years that left her sad and troubled. She stated with tears, "I'm afraid I'm going to lose him." Sophie was the oldest of four children and was one of those who had been taught to always put the welfare of her siblings first, to always obey her elders, to always be available to support her busy mother, and that her feelings were not important. Her parochial schooling had reinforced her code of obedience and a belief that suffering was going to insure her a place in heaven. It had never occurred to Sophie to defy these childhood teachings or to question them with her adult mind. In fact, she had been very careful to suppress any doubts about her family belief system out of a fear of rejection and disapproval.

Sophie was a very beautiful, intelligent woman, yet she was truly surprised when a fine young man courted her and won her hand when she was twenty-one. Eric had been an only child and saw not only the beautiful woman but recognized her kind and generous nature. He recognized that she came from a family with very close ties, but he never realized that those ties were actually knots which held Sophie prisoner to her primary family in ways he could never have imagined. Although his parents had held him close in his early childhood as their only offspring, they had clearly set him free to discover his own belief system and to experiment with various ways of seeing the world with its political, religious and scientific aspects intertwined. As a result, Eric assumed everyone was as open as he was to accepting many points of view as to the meaning of life and how the world worked. He was taken by surprise when he saw the rigid, unquestioning view of the world that this woman whom he had married lived by, and he was especially alarmed to discover that her first loyalty was to her primary family. As he began to realize the intensity with which she held her views and the limits of his own influence, his discomfort in their relationship grew and he was depressed and angry at the same time. His questioning of her beliefs began to corrode their relationship, and she began to hide her activities whenever they were focused on her family.

Although her parents were pleased with her marriage, they did not expect that it would take their daughter out of her role as helper to their tightly knit family. They only expected that they would have additional help from her fine partner. Even though Eric and Sophie lived several miles from her parents and both held responsible, well-paying jobs, she was expected to talk with her mother several times a day and to be concerned, as she had always been, with the needs of her parents and siblings. She was also expected to join them whenever there was a gathering, or when a family problem arose that confounded her parents. Seeing how their parents controlled Sophie, her younger brother and sister had become increasingly independent and disrespectful of their parents. So Sophie was constantly being asked to stop at the family home after work to settle on-going arguments between her siblings and their parents.

She and Eric were also expected to join the family for every Sunday dinner, helping in food preparation and staying until the last dish was dried and the crumbs swept from the kitchen floor.

At first, Eric was charmed by the hustle and bustle of this Italian family so unlike his experience in being an only child. On Sundays, he waited patiently, discussing world affairs with Sophie's father, while she put away pots and pans in the kitchen. After a year of following this pattern, Eric began to chafe and suggested to Sophie that they might spend more time in their own home. At first, Sophie tried to convince him that she owed it to her parents to continue the Sunday dinners and he grudgingly continued to follow her there in order to have some time with his wife. Sophie increasingly began to hide the frequency of her mother's requests that she stop by on her way home from work. Soon she began lying to her mother, telling her that she had to work overtime so she couldn't come by. At the same time many tensions began to develop between Sophie and Eric. They had so little free time to enjoy their own home and each other's company. Sophie became more and more agitated as she tried to balance her love for Eric and the demands of her parents, often subsiding into tears of frustration. Eric found himself uncharacteristically reduced to raising his voice in anger as he saw her struggle to be the obedient daughter her parents had successfully trained to accept their absolute authority.

The balance of power observed in her parents' relationship had never been questioned and Sophie followed her mother's model of acquiescing to her husband's wishes, never recognizing that her mother had survived by adopting passive/aggressive behavior. The only tool she had found to express her anger was to lapse into silence, which sometimes lasted for several days. Since her mother's model did not include open conflict between family members, Sophie had adopted a survival mechanism of "blanking out" when her husband's frustration and loss of patience resulted in his shouting that he couldn't deal with her family any more. Dissolving in tears, she would fold within herself thinking, "I'm a failure—this is all my fault."

Both of them were frightened at the possibility that this on-going conflict would end their relationship so they would step back from any further communication for hours or sometimes days as Sophie had seen her parents do. Together they sought out counseling when Eric declared he was no longer willing to have Sophie's time monopolized by her family. The realization that her partner was not willing to follow the course of action she felt was "right" and which had always won acceptance by the authority figures in her life, caused her to panic.

In a very short time, within the safe environment of the therapeutic setting, both were able to see that Sophie had missed out on developmental stages of childhood and had been terrorized by her father's tyrannical domination and the teachings of the Church regarding sin, punishment, suffering, guilt and sacrifice. In her youth she moved between two extreme roles—that of a frightened, immobilized child and that of a "parentified" daughter with adult responsibilities in caring for her siblings. It was no wonder she was incapable of responding to the family conflicts as a confident adult and refusing her parents' constant demands that now faced her.

It took many sessions for Sophie to develop a trust in herself and to consider the possible changes she could make to enrich her marriage. Letting go of the old scripts of misplaced authority made her feel frightened and insecure. She came for therapy by herself several times to explore her feelings towards her parents and also towards Eric. It was helpful when she began to recognize that her child ego state, as opposed to her adult ego state, was in the driver's seat. It was with both tears and laughter that she saw the necessity for leaving her childhood loyalties behind. It was clear to her that her love for her husband outweighed the need for approval from her parents.

She recognized the need to become aware of the mental activity which kept repeating admonitions from her childhood such as "You owe us," "How can you be so stupid?" "Don't play the martyr," "We're not interested in your drama, get busy." Slowly she began to reject these admonitions and replace them with her adult voice saying "It's okay to share your emotions" "You are a good person and its okay to feel good about yourself." "Your inner voice is important to you and you must listen to it." At first, the concept of loving and listening to herself was so foreign that she dismissed it as not possible. Her first attempts to set boundaries with her family were met with openly hostile threats and the declaration that she was a bad daughter. They threatened that she would be cut out of the family if she did not show up when requested.

Having clarified the underlying issues, both Eric and Sophie felt empowered and ready to make the changes necessary to protect their relationship. Both of them saw the contrast in Sophie's "inside/outside" selves and realized that she faced a major challenge in bringing them together. Her "outside self" was a very valued employee where she was seen as a smart, management-level figure in a thriving company. She stood up for herself with higher management and earned their respect in implementing procedures that contributed to the company's success. However, in the home setting, her "inside self" reverted to the little girl who was fearful of rejection when she didn't please.

With much support from her husband and her counselor, Sophie began to acknowledge her growing resentment. Instead of silencing it she learned to allow herself to "change her mind" or to recognize which voice of authority she was obeying. Sometimes the voice was that of her mother, sometimes her grandmother, and frequently she heard the voice of a nun she had feared in the second grade. Sometimes she would go ahead with old familiar behavior, but in order to do that comfortably she changed her mental script by saying, "I choose to do this," thus over-riding her childhood authorities.

She learned to listen for words in her head indicating external authority such as "should" "ought," "must" " have to"—and when she heard those words she would ask the very important question, "Who says?" Eventually she realized that it was okay to love herself enough to make decisions with her own center as authority.

Her parents complained to other relatives—grandmother, aunts—and tried to enlist them as critics of Sophie's newly discovered independence. Sophie found this very hurtful and asked Eric to signal her when he saw her "caving" to outer childhood authority and she was astounded to find that she did this in many environments without being aware of it.

One day Eric came home with the announcement that he had been offered a very attractive promotion in another state. He dreaded Sophie's response, knowing that her attachment to her family would make it difficult for her to move away. He was surprised and pleased when Sophie declared that she saw nothing keeping them from accepting his job opportunity and that they might find it a wonderful adventure to put some distance between her family and the tensions that still existed. Because she and Eric had presented such a united front and she had so successfully internalized authority, her parents reluctantly acknowledged their preparation to move to another state. Time and time again they reverted to ill-concealed attempts to make their "ungrateful" daughter feel guilty, but their ploys were no longer working. The parents realized that there were only two choices. They could lose Sophie completely or accept their daughter's marriage and her loyalty to her husband. They no longer were being given the authority to direct her life but could continue a relationship with her when opportunities presented themselves.

The difficulty all of us must face in disempowering our childhood beliefs means constant vigilance and the risk of alienation. We are more prone to stay in a familiar box, even though it is uncomfortable and unrewarding, than to go through the process of change. Sophie's change required a period of mourning where she accepted that the world of family relationships was not as she had been led to believe. However, with courage and perseverance, she eventually found herself in a new and comfortable belief system that brought great rewards. In time, this new system gave Sophie new strength, excitement, and a powerful sense of taking responsibility for her life. Instead of wishing only for peace and quiet, she now looks forward to any challenge life might present.

Now instead of giving authoritative adults from childhood precedence over the "still, small voice within," Sophie firsts asks herself about her own feelings in making decisions. She is comfortable with the First Commandment which clearly states that it is our love and respect for our unique self which allows us to return our gift to the world. She saw that she must travel her own soul journey and not that of the family from which she came.

CHAPTER VII

MARRIAGE IS A LABORATORY

Nowhere in life is the phenomenon of the "inside—outside" self more evident than in all committed relationships. Although many, many words have been written about the hard work required to sustain a harmonious yet dynamic marriage, little has been said about the four to six people in the marriage relationship, not counting children. Each of the partners is basically two people, the outside person being the one most evident in the courting stages, while the inside person is the one we discover slowly in the intimacy of commitment and marriage. In addition, we must count the four parents of the couple, remembering that we inherit not only physical genes and chromosomes, but we also inherit behavior patterns and thought patterns without knowing that they are not universal. In other words, it is not possible to really "know" another person until varied experiences bring forth all six people, which can provide a laboratory for growth and a push toward consciousness in both spouses.

It seems I have always known the romantic story of my parents' courtship and marriage. Upon returning to Wisconsin from WWI, my father was greeted with the crushing news that his girlfriend had married his best friend. In his pain and rage, he left Wisconsin to join one of his brothers in Idaho in the very small town of Elk River. He noticed that the lumberjacks, who camped up in the mountains cutting timber, would send someone into town to purchase replacements for torn or worn out clothing, subsequently hauling it back to the camp. With the extensive skills of his "outside self," he quickly rented a small shop, began stocking suitable clothing for lumber jacks and hired a string of mules to lug the clothing directly up to the camps where the men could pick clothing of their choice. His success in his business enterprise was a direct reflection of his success as a student and the necessity of strict management on the farm in Wisconsin. He had experienced many valuable lessons with both his inside and outside selves early in life.

My father's popularity in the small lumber town was instant, and he was sought out by many mothers who saw him as a perfect "catch" for their unmarried daughters. In the meantime, he spotted a young woman across the street from his clothing shop who worked at the soda fountain in the drugstore. In a very short time, he courted her, married her, and began a family. One would assume, if one followed literature and Hollywood dramas, that they had found their "soul mates" in short order and lived happily ever after. Not so. While we embrace the myth of finding our "one and only," we ignore the reality that there are many reasons we are drawn, or magnetized, to another person, most of which are unconscious. Since my father's "inside" self reflected his parent's early deaths and the deprivation in his own life for warmth and nurturing in the family setting, his two selves were starkly different. He had no model for the marriage relationship and the affection between a husband and wife upon which to draw.

In my parents' case, the magnetism had to do with the remarkable physical similarity between my mother and his lost love in Wisconsin. Twenty five years after his flight from Wisconsin, my father took my mother, my brother and me to visit his childhood home. The townspeople held a reception for us. My mother had told me the story of his betrayal upon returning from war and when I was introduced to his former love, I was struck by the remarkable physical resemblance between my mother and her. Seeing this marked similarity between the two women, I realized that the magnetism he had felt toward my mother was perhaps partly explained by their similar physical appearance.

I had always been puzzled by the great dissimilarities in my parents. My father had seemed a serious scholar, always continuing his desire to learn, while my mother exhibited little interest in the outside world. This was partly explained when I learned that she was taken from school before receiving a high school diploma and her very large family was ruled by strict religious beliefs and an alcoholic father. My father's intense interest in his community led to many positions of leadership while my mother was content to pursue her domestic chores and raise her children. I was often struck by his impatience with her as he attempted to dialog about his activities outside the home. His conversation was met by patient attention but very little verbal response. I realize now that she felt inferior because of her lack of education and felt overshadowed by him. Their marriage was held together by a common devotion to four children, a need for respectability and what seemed to be a satisfactory sexual relationship. However, as was true in many relationships in their era, there was little or no observable display of affection between them.

Having observed my own parents' marriage, I was not surprised that marriage brings with it the continual lessons of discovering those two selves, inside and outside. How can marriage not be a gamble when we believe that the one we have fallen in love with in the outside world, played with, worked with, shared with, turns out to have many unknown facets of "inside self" that cannot be known in courtship. Even couples who precede marriage with a long term live-in experience retain guarded self disclosure until the commitment becomes formal. Often the development patterns of relating as single people are hard to change after marriage. Frequently their seemingly clever test of living together before marriage results in too many surprises when the "inside" self relaxes after commitment.

When the gap of character and maturity between the two selves is minimal, discovery and adjustment go smoothly. But when the gap is enormous, the shock of discovery can make the adjustment to marriage a nightmare. UNLESS the reasons for the original magnetism are made conscious, there can be much confusion when romance fades. The marriage is best seen as a laboratory for two individuals to grow and evolve into two fully realized persons, learning to communicate, compromise, or negotiate the differences in their life views. When one or both resist the opportunity for growth and change, the marriage usually ends or results in years of unhappiness for both parties.

Frequently we are drawn to a person because he or she represents a part of ourselves that is latent or repressed. We are unaware that the reason we feel so good with them is that they complete something in us, and we feel whole when we are with them. Or, as was the case with my parents, when the physical appearance meets a desired criterion, the projection creates a total blindness to other incompatibilities important to a long term commitment. After deciding we need to spend the rest of our lives with that person, we draw a circle around the relationship called marriage. The safety within that circle allows us to pull back and view our partner more objectively. Frequently, the first fault we find in our "soul mate" is the very thing that drew us to them. It is usually that buried part of our self that we have either rejected or left undeveloped. Learning to live with it out in the open in the form of our loved one can be challenging. Discovering that the qualities we have projected on the other person are non-existent or had been displaced from another source, leaves us struggling to find a way to "make the marriage work."

The principles of masculine and feminine are equally present in same sex relationships and the more recent opportunity for same sex marriage has presented gay couples with an opportunity for growth and fulfillment in their daily lives. When children are added to the family constellation, the new responsibilities can make it even more imperative (as it does for heterosexual couples) to grow and expand their consciousness.

As if all of those "unknowns" weren't enough, we are also slowly made aware that there are major differences between male and female that no one mentioned throughout the emergence of feminism, the sexual revolution, and the pursuit of equality between the sexes. Since our conscious evolution in these areas is still ongoing, I can only present an incomplete view of those differences.

FOR WOMEN

About men

A little knowledge goes a long way in deciding if he's the right guy for you. First, remember that his brain is wired differently than yours, and if you expect him to be as verbal as you are, you're in for disappointment. A little known fact is that when we are in utero, when the fetus starts differentiating sexually at about five weeks, the verbal area in the brain of the female fetus develops three times faster than the verbal area in the male fetus. Men never had a chance to keep up with our verbosity. We also have a higher vibration (a fast heart rate in a fetus is believed to be a girl while a slow heart rate is predicted to be a boy) and women often move faster in their daily function. We need to give men time to speak and we must slow down our pace when we work together. These differences in masculine/feminine principles are important in the survival of the human race and are expounded upon in Jungian theory. In the feminine principle we are usually dealing with a defused, global consciousness, while in the masculine principle, the consciousness is more linear and exacting. In a healthy marriage, knowing of this difference helps the partners in balancing their energy and speed of activity.

However, there are many men who have been very close to their mothers, or were surrounded by women as they were raised. Those men seem to catch on to what a woman wants to hear and they may sound as though they are your dream come true. The real test is in what they DO. They say all the right things, enthusiastically respond to your verbal needs, sound as if they really "get" you and then lapse into inactivity that will drive you crazy. Don't just listen. Watch! The words don't matter unless they are evidenced in behavior. Because it is often difficult for men to put their wishes into words, it is important to see <u>behavior</u> as a message not to be ignored. It is important that women accept their role as "civilizers" in using tact and diplomacy to address behavior in their spouse.

Many guys are really loath to hurt a woman in any way and "I'll call you" is their way of saying "goodbye." Yet women will sit by the phone for days, never willing to acknowledge the message. If he was interested, he would have called. This avoidance of emotions has usually been modeled by male family members who felt impotent in fixing the pain they might have caused.

It's also important to remember that the "battle of the sexes" is not a myth. When you understand our different priorities in relationship, it's no wonder there is conflict. Most males agree that the following list is accurate (in this order).

1. He wants SEX.

    This isn't their fault. They are biologically set up with a strong sex drive so they will fulfill creation's need to keep life going on the planet. They are driven to impregnate the whole herd. (That's how primitive this drive can be.) Also, men are surrounded by far more visual erotic stimuli than women, not the least of which is a woman's physical beauty.

2. He wants a beautiful woman on his arm.

    This shows the world that they have successfully captured the "fair maiden." It validates their masculinity.

3. He wants domestic support.

    This means they like a cozy, soft place to land after fighting the bears in the outer world, with food prepared and clean socks for the next venture. After all, isn't this what Mother did? When a woman complains, "He's just looking for a mother," she is partially right. If he was raised by a "stay at home" mom, he will have greater expectations for the quantity of the service provided than if he had to help out with domestic chores as a child. There is great change going on in this area since many women hold full time jobs outside the home and many men have discovered the satisfaction of domestic activities.

4. He wants companionship and intimacy.

    Too often the word "intimacy" is thought to be related to sex. A more workable definition is: Knowing what you feel and being willing to comfortably share your feelings with another person. Obviously, this creates a certain vulnerability and if there is hostility in a relationship, it may not be wise to be self-disclosing. One must be able to count on his partner's acceptance of those feelings, whether they are understood or not. Also, this is not possible unless both partners share, knowing that the other understands that there are differences in perception and are willing to withhold blame or judgment while those differences are aired. AND we must believe men when they declare, "I don't know what I feel." Too often a boy has been taught to ignore his feelings for so long that he doesn't know where to look for them.

No wonder we have difficulty with our synchronization when the last thing on a man's list is the first thing on a woman's. And the first thing on a man's list is the fourth on the woman's. Not that both don't want sex. But once the man is in the nest, sex becomes something that women often give out of a love and desire to keep them happy ("Stand by Your Man") since the male sex drive is so much stronger. A woman's nesting instinct helps to stimulate her sex drive and helps her want to keep satisfying her partner. If he is a caring sex partner who understands the differences in their sexuality, this part of the relationship is as enjoyable for the woman, as it is for the man.

Most of us understand that we work from three ego states as far as our behavior in relationship: the child, the adolescent, and the adult. The male and female ego needs also present fertile grounds for conflict. For instance:

1. In the child ego state.

    The male wants to feel taken care of. Yes—as we mentioned before, he does want some mothering, but unless it is so extreme that it indicates a stage of arrested development, it's not a problem for most women.

2. In the adolescent ego state.

    The male is very focused on sex. Surprise? He wants to feel sexually powerful and be sure that his partner looks to him for all her sexual needs, which he satisfies.

3. In the adult ego state.

    The male wants her admiration and respect for his work in the world and verbal validation of his skills. It is a mistake to pair with a man whose work in the world does not meet your value system. A partner's lack of respect can gradually erode his own self respect and interfere with many dynamics in the relationship.

The process of relating to the opposite sex is inherently conflictual, but worth every ounce of energy we put into it. Unfortunately, many men can be confused when they are approached by a woman willing to participate in the initial stage of sex as a gymnasium in order to win his attention. This stage can sputter and die shortly after the initiation which can result in his searching for another gymnasium.

A note of caution; everyone is capable of change, but not everyone is willing to change. If, after close attention to the process of relationship, there is no interest in growth or change, move on. As Dr. Phil says "A relationship may not be change worthy" for you, and the sooner you admit it, the sooner you can move on to find one that is.

We need to take responsibility for where we let ourselves "fall in love." Before that happens, it is a good idea to find out if our standards, values, and goals are similar. It has been said that there are 10,000 "one and onlys" out there for you. He's just waiting to be found. A woman should not waste years of believing the myth that there is one "soul mate" for her. If she finds one she wants to believe is her "one and only," she must not depend on her love to change him. It cannot change him unless he wants it to.

FOR MEN

About Women

One of the first things for a man to understand about women is that they are sexually stimulated by their surroundings, atmosphere and the attention of a man. Many fairy tales play out the theme of the white knight waking the sleeping princess. This is a direct referral to the power of a man to awaken desire in his fair maiden. Her sexuality, whether because of immaturity, inexperience, or from having been "shut down" by unhappy encounters can literally be "put to sleep" until awakened by a suitor who is willing to patiently court her. This is why most books on human sexuality emphasize the difference between men and women when it comes to foreplay. While it usually takes very little to arouse sexual interest for a man, her arousal may need to start in the kitchen with a kiss on the neck. This can be followed by complimentary remarks about her appearance, interest in her activities, touching, helping out, or performing whatever acts of tenderness are known to make her feel loved.

There have been many couples who relate the same "problem" when they arrive for marriage counseling. He is unhappy with the infrequency of her initiating sex in their relationship and she is angry that he doesn't talk to her about his thoughts and feelings.

When a man is able to understand the enormous power he has in rekindling their original enthusiasm for sexual activity, the marriage enters a new stage of enjoyment and maturity for both of them. Sometimes the solution is as simple as taking more time on a daily basis to communicate their feelings about their individual lives and to go to bed together so that there is time for "pillow talk." Other times the solution is in running away from the humdrum pattern of their daily lives on a regular basis. Going away can give them space to rediscover the original moments when they were magnetized toward each other.

Married couples who have "dates" and romantic episodes on a regular basis are found to have much healthier marriages than those who do not. Too often these plans are left in the woman's hands. She may feel tired of being the "social secretary" while he feels his sexual needs are not important to her. She would also like him to talk to her more and to share his feelings. Men who want a flourishing marriage relationship will try to develop their verbal skills. As earlier noted, women have a head start on verbalizing while men have a head start on intellectual, linear thinking.

But most importantly, these couples need education in how differently they experience erotic stimuli. Communication is key in letting your partner know what you are feeling and what you expect of them. Too often a woman will declare, "If he loved me, he would know what I want." The man will look frustrated, declaring, "She said she liked daisies and I've been bringing them to her every Friday." Her retort that she would prefer a single rose occasionally comes as a complete surprise to him. Some women feel that having to be specific about their wants takes the romance out of it. But men cannot "divine" what their partner wants. If she chooses the right moment to tell him what that is, he will not only be able to please her, but be pleased with himself.

Women almost universally agree with the following order as to what they want in relationships although there are changes coming as a result of evolving equality issues.

1. Women want companionship and intimacy.

    (You may remember that this was the 4th priority for men.) When couples come to the office, the woman will often complain that the man never talks to her and the man will complain that she never stops talking. As was pointed out earlier, intimacy requires that they know what they feel and are willing to share that with their partner.

    Because of their great need to talk, women look for a man who is willing to have discussions about even the most minute details of life. If their partner doesn't understand the different priorities of the sexes, his silence can cause some hard feelings. The best solution is, as usual, communication. In the movie "Shirley Valentine" the heroine solved this by ignoring her husband's lack of attention when she arrived home and enthusiastically greeting the house with "Hello, wall."

    Acknowledging the difference in communication needs and agreeing on ways to deal with it can stop the friction. When understanding has been reached, a man can listen and respond as long as he can tolerate, then declare, "I need a 'time out'." An understanding wife will respect this honesty and act accordingly. Good feelings and a sense of closeness are the result. Too often, a man will try to fix his wife's problems, when all she really wants is his acknowledgment that she has been upset and to know that she has been heard. This need is easily met with responses such as, "You really were disappointed, weren't you" or "I think that was frustrating for you." She does not need to have her problem "fixed." She just needs to have her problem heard.

2. She wants a man who is comfortable in the world, and can go out to meet the struggle of earning a living with some degree of success.

This need is not on a man's list although there are some serious changes going on in our present culture. Some men marry a woman with a high paying job and have an expectation that she will always continue to bring home a salary, forgetting that women frequently find motherhood more satisfying than they had believed it would be. If this has not been discussed when comparing their standards and values, it can cause deep rifts. When a woman who had been a bank president expressed a desire to stay home with their newborn twins, her husband felt betrayed and panicky at the loss of income. It was not too long ago that women were expected to stay in the home and the only breadwinner was the husband. Now it is not unusual for a woman's salary to equal or even exceed that of her husband's and if the couple has not explored the feelings involved around that issue, they should.

I have been pleasantly surprised to work with two or three couples who have faced this dynamic and have agreed to have the man take on the role of "house husband" while the woman continues her rewarding role in the world of commerce. Surprisingly, although they are comfortable in this arrangement, they often face criticism and doubt from family and friends.

3. She wants domestic support.

Both parties in the relationship put this desire as their third priority, although it means something different in each case. While some single women learn to shoulder all the responsibilities of home, most married women still expect to give the man responsibility for the automobiles, the yard, home repairs, and garage organization with a shared responsibility for child care, including dressing, bathing and play. A surprising number of men have learned to enjoy cooking, even to the point of partially or totally taking over that household activity.

4. She wants sex.

    Yes, she does. Not as frequently as a man (although there are exceptions to this in the courting stages) but once a stable, frequent pattern of sexual activity has been awakened in a woman, she will be devastated when it is lost, whether through death, by a painful divorce, or the occurrence of an affair.

As with the priorities in a relationship, the male and female ego needs are met in different ways.

1. In the child ego state.

    The female wants a man to be strong and to be a leader so that she can play "daddy's little girl" on occasion. Mostly, she wants to feel special and cherished.

2. In the adolescent ego state.

    The female wants verbal affirmation of her beauty and an appreciation of her body since she learned early in life that male attention mostly started with her development of breasts and hips. She wants notice of her new hairdo or a new outfit and she can feel angry and rejected when changes in her appearance go unnoticed.

3. In the adult ego state.

    The female wants respect for her thoughts and feelings which comes from verbal communication and affection. You may have noticed that this need did not appear anywhere on the list for male ego states.

Working on communication, cooperation, compassion for your differences and developing the skill of capitulation can promote growth in both parties and create an unspeakably valuable lifestyle which frees a man and a woman to pursue their talents and desires in other areas of life.

We marry because we need that one person who will care about everything—the good things, the bad things, the fun things, the mundane things—all of it. We need someone to witness our lives—to care about where we are and when we're coming back—to share what happens with both the "inside" self and the "outside" self. It is a process that results in two people who may have met as halves becoming whole, holy, and wholesome. Marriage is a laboratory in which experimentation, exploration and persistence pay off. It is something worth working for and results in a rising consciousness that gives life meaning.

BACK AT THE OFFICE

Melanie came to the first session by herself, declaring that her marriage was dysfunctional and that she had no idea how to make her home-life more bearable. Her husband, Bob, had recently retired from his successful career in a high tech industry. After thirty years of marriage they found little in common. Bob was spending many hours a day on the computer, trading stocks and managing his extensive holdings in real estate. Melanie had taken a part time clerical job in order to get out of the house. She also wanted some cash of her own because Bob was "stingy and distrustful" of her spending habits.

Their two sons were both doing well in out-of-state colleges.

With some discomfort, she reported that they had not had sex for nearly a year—mostly because she had lost interest with the advent of menopause. She was discouraged because Bob had turned to smoking marijuana again, a habit he had never totally given up since adolescence. Because of her "night sweats" she often slept in another room. She felt that some degree of her lack of interest in sex was due to Bob's controlling nature and because he treated her like a child, telling her she talked too much and that he couldn't trust her with information about the family finances. She had stopped consulting him about large purchases because his answer was invariably, "No." He claimed that his negative response was a result of her overspending, so he decided not to put money in her checking account. He referred to his earnings as "my money."

Another strain had been added to their already stressful relationship by the arrival of her mother from Iowa and the need to help her find lodgings and a competent oncologist to treat her ovarian cancer. Although settled in a comfortable senior residential community and receiving aggressive health care, her mother believed that Melanie should be visiting her more often. She would call Melanie many times a day to complain about her life. She had lost nearly sixty pounds. The doctors were cautious in promising a positive outcome from their treatment of the well-advanced cancer.

We closed our first session with the recognition that there was a great need for relief and that the first step would be to bring Bob to the office. Seeing them together would help in evaluating where intervention might be most effective.

When one spouse begins therapy, it is sometimes difficult to convince their partner to come in. The absent spouse may fear the therapist had formed bias in hearing only one side of the story. So, it was with relief that I saw both Bob and Melanie on the doorstep when they arrived a week later at the office. Bob was very smiley and relaxed while Melanie pushed herself into the far corner of the couch, folding her arms in a manner that suggested she was protecting herself from attack.

After a brief introduction in which Bob asked how long I had been practicing and whether I had children, I began by asking where and how they had met. Bob did not hesitate in telling the story of their meeting at an Eastern college where they shared an interest in coed sports and partying. They began dating and were married six months after they had both graduated.

I asked what had attracted him to her. There was a notable shift in his posture as he leaned forward and described his attraction to Melanie's beauty, her athletic abilities, her high energy and her adventurous approach to life. Glancing at Melanie it was obvious that she found his words surprising. I was aware that his description did not fit the profile she had outlined in our first meeting.

I turned to Melanie and asked what had attracted her to him. She was silent for a moment, still taking in his animated view of his attraction to her. Then, very thoughtfully, she stated that his calm, steady skill in sports, and his very responsible attention to his academic progress had impressed her. Being with him had made her feel safe and anchored. She had liked his willingness to make decisions, but had enjoyed his acceptance of the lightness she brought into his life. She had felt that they balanced each other. Besides that, she added with a giggle, he was tall and handsome.

Neither had been aware that their differences were an opportunity for growth. I began with the obvious possibility that they had both been attracted to a part of themselves that was latent, or under developed. They listened carefully as I pointed out that if I put their descriptions of attraction together, I saw a very whole, fully functioning human being. My suggestion that maybe they had something to learn from each other was met with blank stares. Instead of embracing their differing qualities, they had, as is very common, resisted the quality they were attracted to because it meant a possible need for change or growth in themselves. They labeled dissimilar qualities as right and wrong rather than just "different." Now she saw him as overly rigid and controlling while she had initially seen him as "delightfully responsible" and she had become angry at his attempts to control her "adventurous" approach to life. They had been unaware that they had stepped into the "laboratory" called "marriage" where two people coming together as two halves of a whole can become two whole individuals.

The journey toward wholeness is rocky. It requires change, and in order to bring about growth one must leave the familiar and enter uncharted territory. I call this process the three "Ds." DISGUST, DECISION and DISCIPLINE. Many of us become **Disgusted** with the way we are and the way our lives are progressing and make the **Decision** to change. But unfortunately it often stops there. We can successfully avoid the third "D", **Discipline**, for a long, long time, sincerely believing that our desire for change will bring it about. Not so. Long held beliefs and behaviors do not change without conscious practice of new beliefs and new behaviors.

In the next session we began the process of change by discussing communication. I guided Melanie and Bob through a brief discussion about money, a red button topic for them, in which they were only allowed to tell the other what they <u>experienced</u> in the conflict around money that was so threatening to their marriage. Several times I intervened, pointing out that the speaker was attacking, defending, or going off subject. I had given them a paper outlining specific rules of communication (See Appendix A). One of the most important and most difficult rules is the instruction to use "I" statements and not "you" statements. "I" statements give information about the speaker, while "you" statements praise, attack or criticize the listener.

For example, when Melanie stated "YOU treat me like a child and are unfair when it comes to sharing our money," Bob felt attacked. When she changed her statement to "When you withhold money, I feel like a little child and am angry with you. I hate feeling that way because I want to feel loving toward you." For the first time, Bob understood how his money management made her feel.

One of the major difficulties in learning effective communication in an intimate relationship is the lack of vocabulary to effectively describe your experience. It is helpful to understand that initial communication is most importantly an exchange of information. The reason for giving information about your feelings is that your partner cannot help or understand you without knowing what is going on in your head and heart. Unfortunately, too many of us cannot finish a sentence that begins with "I feel _____." As mentioned earlier, men are often taught as boys to ignore their feelings or risk being called "girlie men." It is sometimes helpful to give the husband a full sheet of words describing feelings so he can begin to identify what is going on inside and communicate the feelings to his wife.

This exercise can only work when both parties understand the rules. Often it is only in the presence of a neutral, guiding party that a couple can make their way toward calm discussion without emotional upheaval. However, the effort brings such amazing rewards that once they have experienced healthy dialog, no one wants to return to the war of words they have habitually carried out. One man took home the rules of communication with the promise to remember them when talking to his family. The next week he walked into the office waving the paper of rules and declared: "I can't follow these rules! It means I have to think before I speak." With a smile, I responded: "What a good idea!"

Neither Bob nor Melanie had allowed themselves to get their emotional or their sexual needs met outside the marriage relationship and neither of them wanted to face divorce. It is very important to establish the truth as to whether there is a third party in a troubled relationship. It can be very difficult to re-kindle love between two people when one or the other has allowed their emotional energy to be drawn outside the relationship. Having settled that there was not a third party involved, Melanie and Bob could call upon all of their emotional energy and could practice the rules of communication for twenty minutes every day. They were instructed to come back for their next session with questions regarding both failures and successes in communication when we could replay their dialog and see where it went off track.

Next, we talked about their sexual relationship and the need to withdraw blame in its dysfunction. Blame is one way of playing victim. When either of the parties sees all of the power "out there" in the other person, they feel no power to help implement change. Both Melanie and Bob displayed a general ignorance about the differences in male and female sexuality. Melanie complained that she needed more cuddling and had stopped touching Bob because it always led to intercourse. His anger flared as he retorted: "All you have to do is tell me what you want!!" I was charmed when Melanie told me on a later visit that a change had occurred and now when she moved over to cuddle with Bob he would turn his head and ask: "Is this Melanie love or Bob love?" When she answered "Melanie love" he would simply turn and wrap his arms around her, much to her satisfaction. She learned that she could respond to his signals for intercourse even when it was not on her mind or her first choice of activity because she wanted to return his consideration of her needs.

As Bob learned that he needed to change some of the black and white rules he had carried from childhood, Melanie learned that she could talk more openly to Bob before making decisions that would affect them both. When she stopped blaming him for her feelings of childlike inadequacy and looked at the source of these feelings in her childhood, she could see them as a direct result of her unhappy childhood. She cried when describing a childhood which was dominated by a non-nurturing father. She worked hard in separate sessions to put down the baggage she still carried from that pain.

A short time later, they learned that Melanie's mother was in the process of dying. It was with Bob's expert managerial skills that they enlisted the help of a Hospice team after moving her into their guest room for her final days. Melanie truly appreciated the calm, organized way in which Bob handled her mother's final wishes, and they prepared for the impending death together. When their sons paid a final visit to see their grandmother, one remarked to Bob and Melanie, "So, what's happened to you guys?" His observation spurred them on to further growth as they realized their sons' future relationships would be influenced with what they were modeling as parents.

As Melanie became more calm and resolved her anger toward Bob, he gave up the habit of smoking pot to please her and they decided together that a glass of wine with dinner would be their only substance use. There were setbacks in their steady climb toward individual wholeness. They were surprised when they discovered that both of them carried childhood pain that had been caused by deprivation of one sort or another. These revelations often ended with laughter or tears. It was a light moment when they looked at each other and agreed that they both had an inner child who needed to grow up. Soon they began to identify their behavior when it was governed by that child, and shifted to the confident adults they were gradually becoming.

Having dropped his escape tools of pot and alcohol, Bob often used Melanie as a sounding board to find a different concept with which to look at life in a more positive, creative way and he came to value the balance that she brought to his daily activities.

When Melanie's mother died, Bob silently held Melanie, listening to all her feelings without questioning, knowing that he could not "fix" her pain. Sometime after the death, they left on a long-awaited "second honeymoon" to Europe where one of their sons was an exchange student. In learning the unconscious reasons for their original magnetism toward each other they were both committed to becoming two fully realized persons, embracing the laboratory of their marriage relationship as the never-ending classroom for such growth.

It is this kind of positive outcome that makes the profession of psychotherapy a great privilege. Time after time there is evidence that we can only proceed on our own soul journey when involved in love relationships. Both the pain and the joy are opportunities for self knowledge, not opportunities for judgment and blame which leave us impotent and bitter. Our entire lives are made up of choices—whether to leave or stay, whether to learn or shut down, whether to be victim or victor. The choice is ours.

Chapter VIII

White Knight/Fair Maiden

It was very early in life that I realized there was a pronounced difference in the way that my brother and I were seen by our parents. I also noticed that my two sisters shared the same grouping I found myself in. We three girls were very close in age and I was the third born. Because the culture was extremely sexist at the time, a third girl was a great disappointment (so I'm told) but when two years later the fourth child was a boy, there was great celebration. The dominant attitude toward my sex was that we be "ladylike" and compliant to the opposite sex. For no apparent reason (to me) my brother was left to experiment with playtime while my sisters and I were given duties in helping our mother at a very early age. We three girls shared a bedroom, while Buddy slept in his own seemingly spacious room filled with toys of his choice. I was also aware that his position in the family resulted in loneliness for him and he was often heard outside our bedroom door pleading in his two year old whimper to be allowed to join us. My heart melted when I heard his plaintive request, "Dirls, dirls, let me in." My older sisters were unrelenting in their insistence at keeping him out and blocked my attempts to open the door and let him in. I felt impotent to stop my sisters' decisions to make him walk behind us and also sit behind us when we went to Saturday movie matinees.

None of us, at that time, had any clue that our behavior was reflecting the model of male/female relationship we saw in our parents and in that historical period. With my present understanding of the balance of power in a marriage, my parent's marriage would be seen as a dominant/submissive relationship.

In reflecting that model, our behavior toward our brother exhibited both a need to comply with the model and a desire to rebel against it.

At Christmas time Buddy was filled with anxiety and often exploded at gift opening time because an expected present did not appear under the tree. We all held our breaths as he was calmed and soothed by our mother, allowing us to return to the ritual of gift opening. Although we three girls never received a bicycle in our childhood, Buddy received one as soon as his feet were able to reach the peddles and I questioned the fairness of this fact openly. I was told that he needed the bicycle because he was a boy. Since it is easier to believe our parents than to question their authority, I began adding a request to my prayers every night "and please let me wake up a boy."

My brother suffered many childhood illnesses and was unable to accompany my father on his endless fishing and hunting trips. So I seized the opportunity to join him and learn the skills of his sports, pretending that I was his son and a part of the masculine world in which he operated. That role so clearly had advantages. What I didn't understand at the time was that my desperate desire to be beside him and copy his behavior was developing a strong masculine principle in myself which would be a determining factor in my choice of a mate in adult life.

Since the ruling need in life is balance, and since both male and female children possess the potential for developing the masculine and the feminine principles, our childhood experiences are powerful influences in that development. In looking back, nearly everyone, regardless of their sex, can see what kind of balance existed as they came out of childhood into adulthood. The lack of respect for the feminine principle characteristics that I observed in my parent's marriage made my choice of emulating and developing the masculine principle very logical.

I know now that all of the feelings and behaviors that I observed and felt keenly at that time were part of the historical era in which I and my parents existed. At that time they were not seen as sexist – it was just the way things were. However, very little was known about the strong influence childhood experience has on the creation of a belief system. **The beliefs and attitudes formed as a child last long into adult life**. Unless attention is paid as to the source of these beliefs and the authority from which they come there can be no added wisdom from individual experience. Self awareness would be limited to "other awareness" and "outer authority." We tend to believe that the world is exactly as we were taught to see it by others who were 100% conditioned by their own experience.

Now that we have learned how differently men and women are wired, it is interesting to look back and see how I met my primitive needs for emotional support given the parents to which I was born. The explanation seems very obvious, once explained, but has been given very little attention in the study of psychology. Carl Jung's contribution ("Memories, Dreams, Reflections" and "The Collected Works of C.G. Jung) in the theories of masculine/feminine principles, or animus/anima, held the key. The child's choice of survival mechanisms is very unconscious. Jung lists both positive and negative examples in both principles. For instance, positive attributes in the feminine principle include global consciousness of relationships between people and world issues, receptivity to homemaking/creating environment, nurturing and serving with heart and intuition. Negatives in the feminine principle include martyrdom, apathetic responses, and deviously fragmented approaches to problem solving which can look scattered and irrelevant. Positive attributes in the masculine principle include specialized, linear consciousness, resulting in analytical faculties, physical courage, leadership and direct action with a focus on facts and political relationships. Negative attributes in the masculine principle include cold, controlling tactlessness, calculating domination, narrow minded arrogance and brutality.

The two principles are complementary when explained that the positive feminine is the guardian of life and queen of the inner world of cause and beauty, while the positive masculine is lord of creation in the outer world of action and strength. If lost in the negative aspects of the principle, the feminine becomes vanity and the masculine turns to brutality.

Inside every little boy there is a "white knight" and inside every little girl there exists a "fair maiden." There are many variations in these mythological, yet real figures, and their existence is usually most evident in relationship with the parent of the opposite sex. There is beauty and danger in this truth. A child can lose a parent of the opposite sex through death, divorce, addiction or mental illness and become caught in a confused projection of adult roles with the surviving parent.

It is clearly seen that when a little boy steps in to save his mother from an abusive father, he has brought forth his "white knight." When a little girl flirts and cuddles with her Daddy, believing that she would be a better wife than her mother, her "fair maiden" is completely absorbed in her success or failure. The troubles begin when the parent of the opposite sex accepts and captures the mythological figure, out of their own desperation, and the child is left without that gift to give to someone of their own generation.

In the experience of my husband's early death, my oldest son stepped up and wanted to fill the role left by his father. He immediately joined me in the kitchen, helping put on meals and took up the task of disciplining his younger brother and sister. His "white knight" was fully engaged. As I observed his behavior, it became important for me to draw a line between his desire to relieve my burdens and his developmental stage. Although I welcomed the help he gave, I turned and suggested that he go get a girlfriend. "I am the mother and parent here and you need to go out in back and play basketball. Be a kid." It was tempting to accept his shining offer to replace his father in both roles of parent and husband. Many mothers unknowingly let this happen because there is such vulnerability after their loss.

If a mother is pushed to become or chooses to be the dominant figure in her marriage and does it with bitterness and resentment, she may act as an abuser toward her husband. A little girl, observing this abuse, will unconsciously play the adoring, pleasing "fair maiden" because the father is a sympathetic figure in her eyes and she will try to protect him. Again, the primal urge is for balance. But the result is the unfortunate loss of the white knight or fair maiden at a developmental age when it may be so implanted that it becomes impossible to retrieve for giving in the appropriate developmental age. This loss can also result in an animosity toward the opposite sex because of an unconscious and inappropriate attachment to their parent. If the opposite sex parent has captured this part of their child, the moment arrives when the child is overwhelmed by puberty and finds the king or queen they committed to are unable to fill their needs.

If the same sex parent is a healthy model of their masculine/ feminine principle balance, the child will model that balance in themselves. If the same sex parent is an emotionally dysfunctional model of their principle, the child may have an unhealthy model and need to balance the two principles at a later time in life. In our present culture, where homosexual couples choose to raise children, the child can be witness to healthy models of both the masculine and feminine principles regardless of the sexual orientation. The development in the child is then determined by the degree to which their needs are met and their own nature.

The dominant/submissive relationship between my father and mother and my high energy nature drove me to imitate my father. I rejected my mother's submissive role and often urged her to stand up for herself. Her fear that I would antagonize my father led her to advise me to "hold my tongue" and "never talk back." This only heightened my determination to get his attention by imitating his behavior. At the age of 10, I stood up to him by declaring "You can't criticize me anymore, because you've never said anything nice about me." My mother was horrified and I was immediately sent to my room to think over my violation.

Given the imbalance of masculine/feminine principles in my development, it was not surprising that as an adult I was magnetized to a man who had a highly developed feminine principle. He had been raised by his widowed mother and five old maid aunts in a home where art, music, and literature permeated the walls. He had been showered with affection and attention to all his needs was a high priority as his mother and aunts vied for his love. As a result, he knew women very well and his behavior was that of a soft, warm teddy bear with six years of college and a great future. I had made up my mind much earlier that I would never marry a farmer who worked fourteen hours a day and fumed over the weather and what it was doing to the crops. For me, Jack was everything that I had never experienced in childhood and, as happens with many couples, I felt more whole and balanced with him at my side.

The same magnetic attraction happened for him when he met a woman who was very attractive to him, but who also was able to function in the masculine principle, for which he had slight modeling. My ability to garden, fix the plumbing and electrical gadgets around the house, never asking for help while re-arranging furniture, were a direct reflection of the time spent by my father's side. With Jack at my side, supporting and adoring me I found the long neglected feminine principle in myself and became a much more balanced person. We were two halves of a whole and he began learning how to hammer a nail and push a lawn mower. This is not always the source of magnetism for couples. Some couples find themselves drawn to a partner so much like them, that their comfort is found in simple "sharing" without the challenge of becoming more balanced individuals in the laboratory of marriage.

After Jack's death, I was both dismayed and grateful as I found myself once again taking on the responsibilities usually acted out by the husband but without the reinforcement of Jack's graceful modeling of the feminine principle. I was well prepared to handle parenting, home and yard maintenance, automobile maintenance and finances. I even went so far as to ask myself (following the theory of Karma) if I might have chosen my parents strict work ethic in order to be prepared for what the future held after my husband's death. It was with regret and some anger that I moved back into my former imbalance of carrying out the masculine principle in order to take on the tasks of a single parent with three small children. It was only later that I focused on continuing my own development of the feminine principle.

BACK AT THE OFFICE

Rachel was referred to my office by a friend whose marriage had been improved with counseling. Rachel seemed very reluctant to reveal the nature of her pain because her husband, Mel, fulfilled every traditional expectation of what a "good" husband could be. She spent the first session praising his success in supporting their family of four and in describing their comfortable home. They had recently spent three days at Disneyland during which he shared many rides with the children, clearly reveling in their enjoyment of the outing. She also reported that he frequently took their son to sporting events, leaving her and her daughter to spend their time shopping or baking his favorite cookies.

The only hint of dissatisfaction came when she mentioned that he did have a lot of hobbies – hunting with his buddies, golfing, and keeping their home maintained with his own handy work. It was only in recording the process notes from the first session that I realized she had not mentioned any intimacy, verbal or sexual, between her and Mel.

She began her second session by confessing that she was not sure why she was coming and didn't know why she should be so dissatisfied when she had a model husband. I began asking questions in order to help her look at the nature of their relationship.

"When do you and Mel talk to each other about your feelings and the experiences you have when you are apart? How often do you and Mel go out to dinner together and re-experience the attraction that brought you together? Do you communicate regarding your differences, or do you avoid any possibility of conflict?"

With each question I observed a fleeting smile but then recognized that what I was observing was an expression of hopeless cynicism. Finally she burst out in anger saying, "I don't bring up anything with Mel that might make him uncomfortable."

"And why is that?" I queried.

"I'm not sure, but it might be that he is tired of emotional discussions and feels women are unable to remain rational if emotions are involved."

"Where did he have that experience?"

"I'm not sure, but it might be because when his father died, his Mother turned to Mel for emotional support."

"Tell me about that."

What followed was a classic tale of a mother who turned to her willing son after her husband's death. Mel was eight years old when his father suffered a heart attack and he accompanied his mother to the funeral home to which the father's body had been moved. He had never talked to Rachel about this experience but she had heard it repeated often by his mother.

"I could never have survived without Mel's strength. He literally held me up when we viewed his father's remains and from that moment on Mel became the man of the house. He was so mature for his age. I probably told him more about my problems than I should have. But he would hold me when I cried until I regained my stability – never walking away and always comforting me with, "it will be o.k., Mom." You are so lucky to have him, Rachel, because he is just the best man in the world."

My heart sank at those words. The first thought forming in my head was, "Rachel doesn't have him." And the second thought was, "His gallantry toward women got very used up when he was a boy." The "White Knight" previously mentioned in this chapter, had ridden out to save the "Fair Maiden," his mother, when he was only eight years old.

Although Mel's mother was in her seventies, it became obvious that she was still his top priority as far as his feeling manly and responsible for her well being. Although he seldom displayed any impatience or anger toward his mother, he did make it clear to Rachel that he had little patience with her need to express feelings. Rachel excused his distancing behaviors with her because after all, he did carry a lot of responsibilities for the whole family and this was his MOTHER. Rachel's belief system was a perfect fit for his behavior, but left Rachel feeling isolated and discounted in her relationship with her husband.

At this point, the therapy turned to education regarding the priorities which result in a healthy or unhealthy family life. In every household there are many entities (or distinct relationships) and each requires the same things. **They each require time for relationship, communication with others, creative activity, reciprocal nurturing, compassion for their differences and respect.** In Mel and Rachel's family there were many entities. Mel, Rachel, their two children, and Mel's mother each needed the listed requirements of time for themselves, inner self awareness, individual activity, nurturing by others, compassion and respect. In addition, there were their relationships to other family members, each becoming an entity with similar needs. In looking at the entities of relationship between Mel and each of his children, it was clear that the needs were being met. This was also true in Rachel's relationships with the children. Each parent was spending time with each child when they could communicate during creative activities and everyone in the family expressed affection and respect for the others.

A determining factor for healthy relationships in families is the priorities set with which these entities exist. At the top of the pyramid of priorities is the executive entity, the mother and father. When the needs for these two known as the "coupleness" are met, every person existing in every branch of the family has a better chance of growing and developing in a healthy way.

As Rachel and I talked, she realized that in their pyramid of importance, Mel's mother represented a stronger role than she did and the "coupleness" was starved for communication, creative activity and reciprocal nurturing. In the most important entity, "coupleness," Mel was choosing to give time, communication, visiting, compassion and mutual respect in his relationship with his mother, but was literally "spent" and unable to give the same to his wife. If this most important relationship fails, and is not at the top of the family pyramid, all other relationships in the family constellation will be negatively affected. Mel knew his wife's belief system included a deep respect for parents and an avoidance approach for causing arguments or any discomfort to others. So for their entire marriage, he had joined and supported Rachel in suppressing her personal needs of intimacy with her husband as she played the dutiful wife.

As it became clear that she was no longer willing to be second choice for her husband's attentions, we strategized as to how to begin change. Withdrawing blame and resentment and acknowledging her participation in this unhealthy relationship helped Rachel process her repressed anger toward Mel. She also felt motivated to display a healthier model of marriage to her children who would inevitably copy what they saw at home in their own choices as adults. This choice sometimes results in a reaction to do the opposite of our parents, or an inability to resist following their model as "right" because they are our parents. **This is one example of the importance of taking back authority from our childhood when we are adults.**

After working on effective communication for a few sessions, Rachel told Mel that she was facing some difficult issues in her counseling and her therapist would like one visit from him in order to speed up her therapy.

Mel's first session with me went rather quickly. His comfort while relating to a woman was evident and he cautiously accepted my suggestion that Rachel might need his help. When asked how they had met and what had attracted him to her, he eloquently described her beauty, intelligence and ability to get along with everybody. But when I asked for his opinion as to why she was seeking therapy, he said he thought maybe she needed more self confidence.

"I believe that you may be the key for her finding that confidence. Do you know that the highest need for a woman in her relationship is to feel "special" and "unique" to her partner? What do you do that would make her feel special?"

Mel seemed puzzled by my question and slightly irritated. "Well, I make a good living and I'm a good father," he answered.

"I think you missed my point, Mel. What makes a woman feel unique is found in the time she spends alone with her partner and in his continuing admiration of those qualities that first attracted him. In other words, "Do you still court her in any way?"

Mel chortled and leaned back on the couch, throwing one arm over its back as he looked out the window. "I don't think you understand how busy I am in my work, with the kids and taking care of my mother."

"How much of your time do you give to your mother?" I asked.

"Well, Mother's had a hard life. My father died when I was eight and she had to raise me and my little brother all by herself. She's in pretty good health for a seventy eight year old, but she still gets lonely and is not very good with managing her finances."

"Does your brother help her too?

"No, they don't get along very well. He gave her a lot of trouble when he was a kid. I think it was his way of trying to get attention because he felt I was her favorite."

"I think you are very wise. We all need attention. Let's get back to Rachel. How often do you take her out to dinner or have a weekend getaway?"

The session ended with Mel's realization that he hadn't had an evening alone with Rachel for a long time and that they didn't ever communicate about their feelings. I thanked him for coming in and asked if he was willing to come once with Rachel to talk about communication.

In a session completely devoted to communication, Rachel was able to tell Mel that she felt unimportant to him and yearned for their earlier relationship when she felt very close to him. In a series of sessions, it became clear to Mel that he felt burdened by his loyalty to his mother and was fascinated to learn that it went against nature to stay so close to a parent. The myths of the White Knight and Fair Maiden made perfect sense to him when examining his childhood and the early death of his father. He took comfort in the truths in literature about "leaving home" and our inability to fulfill our individual destiny when tied to our primary family.

As Rachel and Mel learned to face their true feelings, they found solutions in managing their time so that the entity of their relationship could thrive. Rachel took over his mother's finances and visited her weekly. They appealed to Mel's brother who lived some distance away to find a way to reconcile with his mother and encouraged her to set up activities in the retirement home where she lived.

In our last session, Rachel had visibly bloomed while Mel and she often exchanged glances during the discussion, a most intimate form of communication. They did return a few weeks later to reinforce the steps they had implemented in their new lifestyle. They felt justified in having given money and attention to their marriage issues when they felt a new level of relaxation in their home. Mel reported that his mother was not entirely happy with her son's changes, but that she had reluctantly joined an exercise class and a bridge club at her residence facility. Nothing had been heard from his younger brother.

CHAPTER IX

FEELINGS ARE GUIDES

As children, we are at the mercy of our feelings. How the child reacts to experiences is seen as the child's "nature." Within a single family, we can see brothers and sisters reacting to the same experience in varying ways, depending upon their nature. Some newborns exhibit their nature in the delivery room by what might be called a "laid back" passive nature of contentment while others exhibit a passionate, interactive nature. Since parents are also born with their natures intact, the child might have a very different vibration or energy than its parents. If the parents are focused on power and control, this can set up a lifetime of consternation and conflict because of the differences in nature. Or the child may have a carbon copy nature of a parent and be considered an easy child to get along with.

It was my fate to be born with a very high vibration and a great need to interact with my surroundings. When I was met with deprivation or loving nurturance I responded intensely with feelings of anger or joy. This intensity was counter to my parents' learned methods of calm and reasoned interaction as adults.

Two incident in my childhood illustrate the difficulty my parents had in "controlling" my strong reactive behavior and intense feelings. The resulting clashes and labeling became a part of our parent/child relationship. Sometimes I was seen as a trouble maker with a "temper" and as being too "outspoken." At other times I was seen as a very smart and lively child who led her siblings in many activities.

There was an occasion when I, a twelve year old, was sent to umpire a baseball game at the local sandlot where my younger brother and his friends were spending a balmy Sunday afternoon. He was nine, which means we were in very different developmental stages and we saw the world quite differently. Standing behind the plate calling balls and strikes was something I genuinely enjoyed. I had learned to love baseball because listening to baseball games on the radio and attending the local American Legion baseball games were strong parts of my family experience. Attendance by the entire family was mandated by a father who believed baseball to be the greatest sport in the world. When umpiring my younger brother's game, I called him "out" at home plate when his slide did not beat the ball to the plate. He exploded in anger and rushed at me with a baseball bat. Not wanting to be the victim of his attack, I turned and ran to our nearby home, arriving there a few feet ahead of him. As we raced into the yard huffing and puffing, we found our parents sipping iced tea and enjoying a rare moment of relaxation. My brother dropped his bat and declared that I had made an unfair call that was totally mean and that I was exerting my power as umpire because he was my brother. My father immediately came to his rescue, telling me that I should have favored him because he was my brother.

In my childhood script, which was black and white, I knew this was wrong and told my father he should not "baby" my brother by changing the rules. My father then leapt from his chair in anger at my insolence. It was rare that I saw my father lose control and in my fear I fled, reaching my bedroom just in time to slam the door in my father's face. My mother looked on in horror from the yard as we were both consumed by overwhelming anger and frustration.

In the above incidents, the individuals felt they were justified by different beliefs about what "should" have happened and instead of taking a "time out" we acted on the feelings surging through our nervous systems. Instead, we felt our feelings were "caused" by the other person's behavior. **We were unable to see that the feeling we experienced was telling us about our own experience and belonged to us and no one else. The feeling we had was a guide to call our attention to an inability to accept an opposing point of view.** Needless to say, I suffered severe punishment for such an outburst. I was harshly scolded by my mother for upsetting my father, grounded for several days and alienated from my father for several weeks.

The second incident which reveals the difficulty my parents had with me occurred a short time later. The drama teacher who directed school plays in the 9th grade decided at the last minute to switch my understudy friend to my part as the lead in the play, a role I had coveted. I was stunned. I arrived home just before collapsing in tears, leaving my mother desperate to know the source of my obvious pain. My sense of rejection, resentment and sorrow at having lost my role were so overwhelming that it was some time before I could explain the feelings she helplessly observed. In the meantime my father arrived home and ordered me to stop being silly, to dry my tears and help out in the kitchen. The unspoken message in many of our family episodes was that feelings were not important, or in other words, "stop feeling." In this instance I was surprised when my mother defended my pain and in a rare burst of defiance towards my father, raised her voice, telling him that he just didn't understand how difficult the rejection I had suffered at school was for me.

At the age in which I experienced the event on the baseball field, my black and white world of childhood required that all rules be followed to the letter. I was unable to call him safe even though he was my brother, when he was clearly out. My father, always defending a son who was not as strong as his sister, wanted the rules to be ignored for his son's benefit. It was long after both experiences that I discovered the creative wisdom to be gained from our feelings. Both my brother's and my father's responses in these incidents were based on their own special "script" of "fairness and justice" and came from the rules they had formed from their own life experiences. The fact that we all had such strong emotions accompanying our idea of what was "right" resulted in angry responses and a negative outcome for everyone. My father's inability to understand my painful sense of rejection regarding my role in the school play was based on his belief that an emotional response was weak and unnecessary.

Too often we have been taught to give others the responsibility for our feelings and use phrases such as: "they hurt my feelings," "he made me angry" or "she drives me crazy." In reality, no one else "causes" our feelings. Someone else's behavior or an external event evokes a feeling response in us, but the feelings are ours and are a very important message to us about our own view and our beliefs about right and wrong. Not only are our feelings an important message to us, but different feelings carry different messages that, if examined, can guide us to appropriate, creative behavior. As we mature, we have less need to express our feeling immediately or inappropriately and can strategically respond to our emotion after processing its energy.

Anger is the feeling we experience when something is not going the way we want it to. It is a natural emotion but acting in anger is nearly always destructive. Many times in the role of therapist I hear this statement answered with, "But nothing ever gets done in our house unless I explode in anger." The reality is that while the explosion may get the job done, it leaves in its wake fear and resentment. To get desired responses through creating fear or resentment means that fear and resentment become a part of the family dynamics and are internalized. Both emotions, when kept inside the body, cause the unhealthy constriction of body processes. Most people will carry those strongly stored emotions into adult life, and unless they are recognized as learned emotional baggage, they will be experienced as the way the world is and with inappropriate responses in adult life.

Also, we need to identify the part of the body where we first feel anger. It might be in the jaw, the neck, in increased heart rate or clenching fists. If we become aware of where our body calls attention to the arrival of anger, we have the opportunity to block an angry, destructive response to whatever is happening. What most people have not discovered is that our body is a very reliable instrument for giving us messages about ourselves. It is not interested in what is going on outside of us, but it is working 100% of the time as a guide for our, and only our, well being.

Anger has an important place in our psychic, emotional experience but the adrenalin rush that it brings has carried us into many an unnecessary conflict. These conflicts can end in destructive behavior, violence and even war and killing.

What is perceived visually or audibly is registered in the central nervous system, but not always interpreted correctly there. Our central nervous system is headed by the brain which contains all the rules, regulations, attitudes, self image, beliefs, and decisions which we have gathered in our lifetime of learning to survive. Therefore, we cannot always trust our mind to give us an unbiased and objective message about what is going on. When our body reports the feeling of anger, our mind is busy sifting through years of information and looking for an interpretation or perception that fits our belief system. We may hear in our head a long-held rule that tells us, "You have to hit back when someone attacks you verbally or physically." In our adult life this may be seen as a very immature response— one that does not consider time out, diplomacy, or other less violent, more creative reactions. Our body is 100% reliable in reporting an emotion. As a matter of fact, our body experiences the feeling before it is registered in our mind and can guide us in being aware of the emotion in time to choose our reaction.

Negative feelings become a health issue because they constrict the body processes, causing blood vessels to narrow, forcing the heart to work harder to maintain adequate circulation, tightening chest muscles and thus causing shallow breathing, depriving the body of adequate oxygen. As these body responses heighten they send the digestive system on a wild search for additional acids to hasten the body's preparation for battle and send out unnecessary adrenalin to stimulate reaction. All of these changes in the body are important processes when primitive physical survival is the goal. However, our evolution has created different circumstances of survival and we must re-examine the place of feelings in our current environment.

Many people believe that they should not experience anger, or if they do, that it means they are "an angry person." This belief can be reinforced by religious education or adult authorities who punish a child for exhibiting anger. It can be very difficult to let go of these incorrect beliefs regarding anger and to see it as a natural and human emotion that everyone has unless it has been repressed to the unconscious.

In the anger management classes I have taught, the statement that anger belongs to the one experiencing the anger brings strong rebuttal. "But I <u>should</u> be angry at lousy drivers" or "Nothing ever happens at home <u>until</u> I get angry" or "I have a <u>right</u> to be angry at what was done to me." In all of these statements, the attempt to justify holding on to anger leaves out the most important fact. When we are in a state of anger, WE are paying the price for whatever has taken place. Our bodies are aging at many times the rate they age when we are in a calm state. Our blood pressure has risen, our bodies have become tense and the brain is not receiving adequate amounts of oxygen. Unless the messages and guidance of the feeling are examined, the price is high. Our feelings are there to tell us about US.

In the personal examples cited previously, my brother's anger was because I had not called his play in the way he wanted it to be called. My father's anger was because I had not bent the rules for my little brother as he wanted me to. My anger was because I felt the rules should be followed. I also felt the drama teacher had made a decision to replace me which was unfair and not what I wanted. In all three cases, we didn't get our own way and experienced the feeling of anger. In all three cases our anger determined our behavior and led to continued negative feelings.

If we are to rescue ourselves from our own anger and take responsibility for it, we need to acknowledge the emotion when it arrives. If we feel our heart rate accelerating or our chest constricting, we need to start an inner dialog which goes as follows:

> I am feeling ANGER.
> Something has not gone the way I want it to!
> Guess what! I won't always get my own way.
> Is this something that has happened before in the human experience?
> So the universe includes jerks, meanies, accidents and ignorance. (This is news?)
> Can I accept the universe as it is, or do I consider it my job to change the universe.

After taking a deep belly breath and releasing the tension in the body, asking the following question can put you on the track to creative response:

Now that I am back in charge—what can I DO about it?

Sometimes the answer to that question is "nothing" and we must detach from the incident. Other times we find creative ways to intervene.

In a state of anger our brain is deprived of sufficient amounts of oxygen to think clearly. For many people who are used to exploding in anger, believing it to be an effective method of getting things done, it is difficult to consider the pause in which they would go over the above internal dialog. However, after years of professional practice with hundreds of clients, I can guarantee that old patterns of using blustery anger as a tool can be changed to a powerful method of guiding our actions with a cool head.

BACK AT THE OFFICE

Cliff was a successful, though exhausted, owner of a thriving company. Doctors had warned him that his high blood pressure would shorten his life if he did not shift his angry and belligerent style of management. Because he had experienced success in his business life, he was reluctant to agree with the doctors regarding his style of management. The only reason he agreed to talk to a counselor was because of their warning about his shortened life expectancy.

Cliff had adopted his method of persecuting those around him with his anger as a result of his father's tyrannical style. He had never made a connection between that style and his father's early death at the age of fifty eight. Cliff agreed to curb his anger long enough to try the above inner dialog, mostly to get his doctors off his back and to be able to prove that his method was the only one that worked. Two weeks later he came back to the office and sheepishly admitted that he had possibly been wrong about his effectiveness as an angry person. He was later amazed at how easy it was to gain others' cooperation when he dealt with his anger before acting. He laughed when he said, "Nobody quite knows what to do with me now that I remain calm and reasonable." But most importantly, Cliff's blood pressure had dropped to normal, and he reported a great increase in energy and enjoyment in his work.

Fear is another powerful and natural emotion that has an important place in our ability to survive.

Fear is a feeling that communicates to us the sensed reality that we are facing some kind of danger – physical, mental, emotional, or spiritual. To ignore our fear is to risk suffering consequences without being prepared to protect ourselves. Frequently, clients have been unaware of their fear because of a script that sees fear as an unacceptable feeling in their adult ego state. When asked, "What are you afraid of?" their initial surprise at acknowledging that feeling is followed by an immediate recognition of the source of the fear.

Often the feeling of fear brings new information about our own vulnerability and can guide us in continued growth and confidence. Fear can also guide us in establishing boundaries that keep us from expending unnecessary energy and depleting our body of energy needed to promote health. In the previous example from my childhood, my fear of my father's anger caused me to run swiftly through the house to avoid his catching me and venting his feelings. It is a mistake to ignore or try to eliminate fear. Fears of falling or of loud noises are feelings that even a newborn responds to. As we mature, our fears become more sophisticated. Some people have a strong fear of rejection or of being alone. Being fearful can be a mark of wisdom, not weakness. But failing to acknowledge this emotion can be a mistaken bravado. It can result in agoraphobia, claustrophobia and more commonly in panic attacks which limit our ability to function.

BACK AT THE OFFICE

When I first met Gracie, I was struck by her delicate beauty and the charm with which she presented herself. She had been told about my counseling practice by a former client whom she trusted, but it was not until the third session that she brought forth her reason for coming for help. She dealt with a constant fear of panic attacks and a sense of vulnerability that had become unbearable.

She had been raised in Iowa until the age of seven when her widowed mother moved herself and her five children to California in search of a new beginning. Gracie was the youngest child, and the move had resulted in a "circling of the wagons" where the children focused on their mutual support. As the youngest, Gracie became the recipient of much care and attention. Because of her delicate physical appearance and her birth order, she was treated as though she was fragile and was told she must always let them help her. She grew up believing that she must be fearful of outsiders and be especially careful not to get lost among strangers. Whenever she ventured into a shopping mall her hand was always held tightly by an older sibling. By the time she was twelve, she thought of herself as weak and vulnerable. She had accepted the family identity of "poor Gracie."

Her memories of childhood in Iowa were especially strong because she had enjoyed a close relationship with her maternal grandfather who made her feel good about herself and who encouraged her to try new activities. Now, while relating her story in the office, she was struggling with a need to fly back to Iowa to see her grandfather, possibly for the last time, but she had not been able to deal with her fears of air travel. In her script, this meant turning her safety over to strangers and having no control. Several years earlier she had begun to have panic attacks, the first occurring at a shopping mall, and had been having succeeding attacks while she was on bridges, near speeding trains, while driving a car or for no apparent reason. Her heart rate would suddenly accelerate; she would feel faint; her palms would become sweaty. In her panic she had to find a place to sit down and wait for the symptoms to subside. As a result, she had developed a deep-seated fear of the panic, or as psychology has taught us, a panic about the panic, rather than a rational fear of the circumstances.

In her present circumstance, Gracie's fear was guiding her to recognition that there was some work to be done in unraveling the childhood beliefs that were in charge of her adult mind. It was relatively easy for Gracie to recognize the source of her panic attacks; however, it took several months and a strong determination on her part to overcome the responses her body had developed to protect and defend her from her irrational fears. Without the strong motivation to pay a last visit to her grandfather in Iowa, she might not have conquered the patterned response of fear that left her weak and confused.

She adopted methods for diverting her mind as soon as her body reported the arrival of fear. After much practice she was able to take deep "belly" breaths, close her eyes and repeat quieting phrases in her mind's ear. She tested her methods by gradually venturing out on local freeways and across bridges. Although there were several setbacks, Gracie felt confident enough to board an airplane with her sister a year later as they headed for Iowa. She reported with flushed triumph that she was now free to go wherever she wished. In our last session, she was planning a trip to Italy with her husband and children. She did not eliminate fear from her life— she triumphantly rose above it when her body announced its arrival.

Resentment is a feeling that tells us we are doing something we do not want to be doing. We must stop doing it or change the belief that causes us to do it. This is an especially exhausting emotion that needs to be processed. Too many times, we do not challenge the teachings of our childhood and keep following them without question. When we follow a rule blindly, fearful of questioning whether or not we agree with it as an adult, we sometimes develop resentment. It is very difficult to stop doing something that you were taught is the "right" way to do it and you are still giving authority to those adults in whom you necessarily but erroneously placed your trust as a child.

The following case frequently presents itself in my clinical practice.

BACK AT THE OFFICE

Marie sat down heavily and heaved a great sigh as she began. A woman of about sixty, she appeared to be very tired with deep lines in her face and circles under her eyes. My first thought was that she must be ill. However, it turned out that the cause of her physical appearance was her resentment toward her mother, a woman of ninety who was confined to a nursing home. Three years before, when it was necessary to move her to the nursing home, her mother had made Marie promise that she would visit her daily. With few exceptions, Marie had kept her promise, but in carrying out her mother's request she had put aside most of her own personal, family and social life. As a result, Marie was filled with unexpressed resentment that was clearly taking a huge toll on her physical health.

As had many in her generation, Marie had been admonished as a child that she owed a great deal to her parents. The Old Testament was frequently quoted: "Honor thy father and thy mother." The New Testament teaching that one must leave their mother and their father to become fully conscious was ignored. So strong was her belief that she "owed" her mother the duty of daily visits, that Marie was presently putting her own health in jeopardy by her efforts. When this was pointed out to her, Marie was at first unable to consider changing her pattern by disobeying her mother's demand. When she suggested to her mother that she might only come every other day, she was immediately reprimanded, and in a pinched whine, her mother declared, "You are a bad daughter." As her therapist I had very little hope that Marie could reverse the lifetime rule which gave her mother authority over her life or that she could save herself from this unhealthy situation.

But, as my clients often do, Marie surprised me and began to see how irrational and unhealthy her behavior had become. In the end, she visited her mother only twice a week and was astonished when her mother established new relationships with her fellow nursing home patients. Had Marie continued to carry her strong resentment, I have no doubt she would have become ill. The only alternative to stopping what she was doing was to change the childhood script that forced her behavior. A new script was created which replaced the admonition "I have to visit my mother daily" to "I choose to visit my mother more than once a week." This changed the authority from a critical outer authority to an inner, nurturing authority which she heard from "the still small voice within" her own center.

In changing her attitude and by internalizing authority, Marie unburdened herself of the feeling of resentment which was weighing her down.

Guilt is a feeling that tells us we are violating or have violated our own standards or those standards of behavior we have accepted from others. Guilt is an important feeling that can help us in discovering where we give authority. Many institutions promoting a dogma of loyalty, morality, and outer authority depend upon guilt to retain authority over their members causing them to follow the institution's programs. If we have accepted the dogma and values of an outside authority, guilt will tell us when this code has been violated and will keep us tied to outer authority. As an important personal guide, the feeling of guilt must be listened to and examined in order to know whether the authority we have violated is our own, or one that has been imposed on us.

Guilt has often been resolved for someone carrying that burden with the simple question: "Who says?" When adults are able to examine the source of the script that judges them as wrong, they often discover they are listening to a voice from their childhood experience. The answer to the question, "Who says?" often turns out to be a mother, father, teacher, priest, nun, or grandparent to whom the child gave authority. **It is the**

responsibility of every adult to re-examine the rules they carry in their head and decide whether they accept that rule as an adult, or can discard it as one that was accepted by a powerless child.

If the adult discovers they still believe in the rule and want to follow it, they must see their guilt as telling them they have violated their own standards and then do whatever they can to absolve the guilt with apology or a decision to stop future violations. They could also feel comfortable in adjusting their standard to reflect their adult beliefs. There are many tools that can be used to absolve guilt when parties who were violated are no longer available. Writing a letter of apology to someone who has died, or accepting the rule, "There are no mistakes in life, only lessons" can help us clarify the lesson and accept forgiveness of ourselves.

BACK AT THE OFFICE

Bill was suffering digestive problems and his doctor suspected that he had unresolved feelings about his recent divorce. The story he told of a tedious marriage where he and his wife experienced little interaction was not uncommon. He expressed sorrow that they had spent several years presenting a picture of the perfect couple to those around them. He flushed as he spoke about his futile attempts to put away feelings of attraction to other women. His wife had buried herself in her profession, and they seldom discussed their relationship or the lack of feeling between them. It was only when he found himself uncontrollably drawn to a fellow worker, who returned his attentions, that he made the decision to ask for a divorce. Surprisingly, his wife quickly agreed and they reached an amicable agreement on dividing their assets and finalizing the divorce.

Several months later, when Bill took his new partner to visit and be introduced to his parents in another state, they were met with a chilling deference that startled and embarrassed Bill. His father took him aside and after closing the door voiced feelings that he declared were shared by the entire family. "How could you divorce Lois? Don't you know no one in this family has ever been divorced? Don't you know you have upset your mother and made it difficult for her to hold up her head? What got into you?" Bill's stomach churned and he hung his head as his father continued to berate him. His childhood habit of giving his father authority brought an overwhelming sense of guilt. He and his partner left the next day.

The question of "Who says?" was very clear to Bill as he began to unravel the script with which he was raised. He allowed himself to admit that he did not believe in the fundamentalist religion his family still embraced and that the period of history in which he existed was far more accepting of divorce than his parents' era. He allowed himself to admit that he had made a mistake in hanging on to his first marriage as long as he had and that the resulting divorce was a life-giving act for both him and his ex-wife. He gave up any expectation that his family could understand or accept his actions, and slowly his stomach returned to health. He continued to relate to his parents as a loving son but gave up sharing his personal life with them. He dropped any expectation that they could understand or agree with his adult behavior. In changing the script by which he lived as an adult, he resolved the feelings of guilt projected on him and accepted the new life he had chosen with his new partner.

Anxiety is the feeling that tells us we are caught in the past or in the future. It has little to do with the moment. Because many of us are caught in the trap of worry, there is a wide use of anti-anxiety medications in our culture. In the moment of acute chaos and confusion, medications can be a helpful crutch, but without talk therapy or self examination in which we examine the script we carry around in our heads, we can be condemned to dependency upon drugs to be emotionally stable.

Lots of attention has recently been given to the need to be "present" or to be "mindful" of the moment in which we find ourselves. Much of our life can be blighted by the inability to focus our attention and energy on the experience in which we find ourselves. Instead, we are preoccupied with what happened in the past or in trying to control what may happen in the future. Although all of these phases of life, (past, present and future) are a part of our consciousness, we can only act in the present. The past can be re-experienced over and over again, but it is not possible to change it—only to learn from it. The future is certain to arrive, but is determined by the choices and plans we are making in the present. Worry, as defined in the dictionary, is to feel uneasy or anxious – to torment oneself with or suffer from disturbing thoughts.

When our thoughts are focused on worry, we cannot be present. In his great wisdom, St. Augustine made this clear when he stated, "I was not with you because I was not with myself." Therefore, unless we discipline our mind to focus on our immediate experience, we can die without having participated in life at all. It is only in the moment that we have a choice in what actions we are taking. That choice might well create the future.

BACK AT THE OFFICE

Anna, the mother of three beautiful children was referred to me by her doctor. She had been using medication to help calm her constant worries and in order to function as a wife and mother. Her friends referred to her as a "worry wart" because she was always bringing up possible dangers and dampening any joy in planning events for their families.

It was not mysterious as to why she was preoccupied in this manner when you heard about her chaotic childhood with a nervous and sometimes suicidal mother. She had lived in a constant state of fear that she would come home to find her mother dead or ranting about the things that had gone wrong in the past. She bypassed many childhood activities, thinking that it was her responsibility to save her mother from harm caused by her constant anxiety and depression.

Anna was highly motivated to gain some control over her negative thoughts when she realized how she was affecting her beloved family. She had a very loving and understanding husband, and all three of her children were thriving. However, the constant expectation that she had done something wrong, or was about to face calamity never left her.

For weeks, after allowing time for her to express the despair she suffered as a child, we practiced coming into the present by looking about the office, settling back in the pillows and admitting that there was nothing to be afraid of or to be responsible for at the moment. She was encouraged to acknowledge that she was perfectly safe in this environment and could trust that anything she felt would be accepted and understood. She was able to "transfer" her need to be in charge, and she expressed the relief she felt in the simplicity of "being present."

In order to anchor this feeling and carry it into her life outside the office, we practiced exercises of relaxation and imagery – imagining herself functioning in the same relaxed manner in every environment with a voice inside her head that stopped negative thoughts when they tried to intrude. We used the graphic metaphor of seeing herself going down the freeway of life and having a choice as to which off-ramps her mind would travel down.

Instead of following signs on the freeway saying, "Anxiety – Next Right" she chose only to go down off-ramps where signs promised, "Joy and Creativity – ¼ mile" "Clear Communication – ½ mile." She relished the truth that she could use an adult voice in her mind to choose NOT to go down negative paths of thought and to see that her mother's life was not her responsibility. Her mother's life was the result of **her** choices. The time between the arrival of negative worries and her ability to dismiss them became shorter and shorter, and although it took many months, she "changed her mind" in ways that brought her into the present. Her family enjoyed her victories so much that they made a family game out of asking each other, "What off-ramp did you just take?"

Positive feelings are also precious guides that add to the enjoyment of being present.

> **Love is a feeling that tells you that you are in a state of connectedness with someone or something else.**

Too often we do not stop to revel in the feeling of love. When gazing at a beloved spouse or watching our newborn child, our body will produce a sudden rush of warmth in the solar plexis area – a sense of expanded relaxation that is our physical response to love. It is often in this part of the body that we are notified of positive or negative emotions. Sometimes we have expressed it as "having butterflies in our stomach" or "feeling like we've been punched" or "oozing with love."

> **Gratitude is a feeling when something or someone outside yourself has left you with a sense of peace or validation.**

While love is the fuel for the engine of life, gratitude, forgiveness and presence are what make for a smooth and rewarding soul journey.

CHAPTER X

PSYCHOLOGY AND
SPIRITUAL TRUTHS

I am well aware of our human desire for answers as to our life's purpose and meaning. Many people in every culture have found answers to their questions regarding origin and direction in institutions claiming the truth. I am also aware of the comfort in settling the questions and the satisfaction of joining an organized group who agree on the answers they have found.

I support the individuals who gather in churches, synagogues, or temples in pursuit of their faith. My particular journey, although circuitous, has led to a satisfying concept of life and death which sustains my faith in the dependability of the universe which is ruled by the laws of cause and effect. Most satisfying has been the discovery that these laws of cause and effect exist at every level of life: physical, mental, emotional and spiritual.

In my studies of religions I have found these laws mentioned in Holy Scriptures in many different ways. When I turned my attention to a search for answers regarding Jack's cancer, using the scale of cause and effect, I began to understand the contemporary state of medical science. Up to that point I had simply leaned on my childhood teachings of God's power to create results based on good and evil. Realizing that humankind had always included illnesses for which they found no cure, beginning with plagues, consumption, polio and now cancer, helped me trace the evolution of science and see the great strides that have been made. It stabilized my trust and acceptance that we have much further to go and that my husband's malignant brain tumor was among those illnesses which science is aggressively addressing.

The fact that cause and effect represents immutable law is most obvious at the physical level. We all know that we cannot jump out of a ten story building and go up. We all know that we cannot turn our backs on exercise and mobility and maintain good health. However, mental, emotional and spiritual laws have only been accepted as we advance our knowledge of psychology, the mind/body relationship and the fact that human spirit exists as an energy, apart from religious institutions. Many people will hasten to explain that although they do not belong to an institutional religion, they are very spiritual.

We do not decide how our emotions and our spiritual state are going to affect the body. This also comes under the law of cause and effect. Slowly we have come to realize that negative emotions cause the body processes to constrict, interfering with digestion, immune function, cardiovascular process and respiratory process. Prayer can change a state of tension where faith is present, but we cannot always be in a state of prayer, and the relationship of feelings to body responses never changes. The laws governing mental and spiritual health require a level of self awareness as to where our mind has taken us and whether we are "down spirited". However, the simple attitude of positive expectancy which accompanies a believer when praying can help the body relax and turn us toward hope. What changed with the positive expectancy was governed by mental and emotional laws. We cannot be depressed emotionally without depressing the body function. We cannot be alert and contemporary unless we are open to new knowledge at the mental level. No amount of declaration regarding doctrine and beliefs can change these laws of life which have not been altered since human life and consciousness began.

At the time when I could have used some psychological counseling in order to deal with the challenges in my life, it was not even a possibility. At that time, it was widely believed that only people with mental illness needed psychotherapy and that only the weak leaned on professionals. In my disillusionment, I had left the comfort of a church community. As a result I felt abandoned, lonely, and alienated from all those around me. I was unwilling to share with others the desperate state of my husband's mental incapacity out of loyalty toward him. It is with some surprise I can now report that a great portion of the help I found some time later came through the teachings of a familiar source for religious worship – the teachings of Jesus. This understanding of Jesus' teachings did not come through a religious institution but from a study group led by a Stanford professor and his wife. Their study was focused on the **mind** of Jesus.

My parents came from two different religious backgrounds, Catholic and Lutheran. My mother had often related the story of their marriage and subsequent arrival of four children. In the small lumber town in Idaho where they lived, religion was taken very seriously. My father made it very clear from the beginning of their relationship that he would never follow Catholic beliefs; so they eloped and returned home to Elk River after a civil ceremony in Couer d'Alene. When they experienced the birth of their first child 10 months later they were paid a visit by my mother's priest who sternly announced that she had given birth to a bastard since they had not been married in The Church. The same Priest arrived after the birth of her second child – admonishing her that she would go to Hell if she did not return to the Catholic fold and seek redemption. When the Priest arrived after the birth (mine) of their third child, my father met him at the door and, as the story goes, threw him off the porch by his collar. In their need to be together without the threat of hell and evil doing, they decided to find a third religious organization in which to educate their four children about the Bible.

Both of my parents seemed to recognize that the institutions in which they were raised had produced a belief system that denied any truth found outside their particular church. In looking back at this insight, I am impressed with their mutual respect for their differences and the decision to help their children choose a place to practice religion, without the burden of imposed dogma, when they were more mature.

They settled on the Presbyterian Church because in visiting several institutions for this important role, they found the sermons there less filled with dogma and rhetoric which declared theirs to be the only and correct belief system. While exposing their children to some form of religious training, my parents also wanted them exposed to a lesser burden than Catholicism and Lutheranism which, in their view, had made sin, guilt, obedience, suffering and fear the focus of human life. Both of them experienced this burden from their childhood religious training.

So it was in this spirit of open thought that they made Sunday school a part of the children's weekly schedule. However, as I approached pre-adolescence, I wondered why my parents never attended Sunday worship. By then I had grown accustomed to memorizing scriptures that rewarded me with new Bibles and lovely paintings of Jesus as a boy.

From my early vantage point, God required very clearly defined obedience. You were to accept that Jesus was His only begotten son. You were to obey your parents, attend services weekly, place money in the collection plate, remain a virgin until marriage, never lie or swear, and love everyone, including the brat next door. In obeying these rules, you were guaranteed protection from all evil and would be welcomed to a place of indescribable beauty and pleasure at the end of your life. My childish and earnest decision to follow these rules guided my decision making in every aspect of my life. After learning that we could be forgiven more than seventy times seven, I quickly forgave myself for any lapse in obedience. When my Catholic friends told me about their required "confession," I usually added a lie of disobedience to my nightly prayers. In the meantime, I attended a youth group at the Presbyterian Church where we roller skated wildly around the church gymnasium, an activity which made the Catholic practice of kneeling in silence seem unappealing. I also sang in the senior church choir when it was declared that my soprano voice was needed in the choir loft on Sunday morning.

Following the wartime death of my high school sweetheart, Doug, and my move to California, I attended a large and beautiful Presbyterian church in San Francisco but did not feel a need to become actively involved. It was a pleasant surprise, upon meeting Jack, to discover that he, too, had been raised in the Presbyterian faith. We willingly followed our belief, were married in the church, and as our three children appeared, had them baptized. In our minds, we did everything "right." Jack and I were deeply involved in church activities after we moved to San Mateo, leading the couple's group, sending the children to Sunday school and summer Bible study. I loyally attended choir practice every Thursday evening and Jack proudly watched me from the aisle on Sunday morning as he passed the collection plate and the choir sang out praises. Together we led a group of Junior High students in Bible study on Sunday night.

Nine years after our marriage, when the tragedy of his brain tumor and subsequent lobotomy shattered our lives, I turned my wrath on the church, God, and the futility of having "done everything right". What kind of God would allow such a merciless illness to befall one of His faithful children? Where were all the promises of protection, love, and inner peace that had been the strength of my childlike "faith"?

In spite of their attempts to support us in our tragedy and much to the dismay of our fellow churchgoers, we gradually withdrew from regular church attendance and I spent all my energy in caring for our three small children and the constant needs of the stranger (my husband) we now lived with. It was necessary for me to take a part-time job at a nearby answering service where initially, I kept my personal life to myself. One day the woman sitting next to me at the answering service switchboard shared the story of her daughter's death from leukemia. When she told me the death had occurred only one year ago, I turned to her in amazement. For several weeks I had experienced her as a very calm, peaceful and happy person. How could that be when she had so recently suffered such a loss?

For the next few weeks, whenever we had a break from the switchboard in front of us, I poured out my own pain and confusion to her.

I told her about my anger toward a God by whom I felt betrayed. I told her I had no belief left in the religion that had been taught to me, but that I still searched in the Bible with a desperate need to find some answers. When I quoted scriptures to her that had been memorized in childhood, her response was often, "Don't you think that Jesus was really trying to say_____.?" Invariably her responses provoked a degree of enlightenment in me, and I saw how the teachings of Jesus actually applied to my current experiences in life. Finally I exclaimed, "Where did you learn this way of understanding the meanings in the scripture?" My curiosity about her religious background brought forth that she had been raised as a Christian Scientist. She, too, had abandoned her childhood religion and she related to me that she had found new faith in life by participating in a group study based on the <u>mind</u> of Jesus.

I can only explain the miracle of our meeting by the law of attraction, but I hurriedly joined the discussion group she recommended where Henry B. Sharman's book "Jesus As Teacher" provided the basis for discussion. Sharman emphasized the use of critical thinking methods employed by advocates of "the higher criticism", when studying the bible. It turned out that the organizers of the study group I had joined were a distinguished Stanford professor, Harry Rathbun and his wife Emilia. They had recently studied with Henry Sharman in Canada where he encouraged the application of the critical methods of historians, scientists, and literary critics to the Bible.

After returning from their seminar, the Rathbuns had begun to share their inspiring experience of questioning traditional religious beliefs. This approach challenged the students to do the right or loving thing regardless of tradition, institutions, or the potential cost of acting against doctrinal edicts. They formed discussion groups which met in their home on the Stanford campus. The groups quickly multiplied and because of the intense interest by the general public, they began training leaders and presenting one and two-week seminars in a wonderful setting in Ben Lomond, California. The people drawn to this examination of the historical Jesus as a teacher were nearly all people who were highly educated and shared my lack of trust in what their childhood religious training had taught them. Professor Rathbun was also known on the Stanford campus for a senior colloquium he taught called "The Mind of Jesus" which drew hundreds of students to his annual lecture in Stanford Memorial Church. The people I met through these discussion groups were a congregation of Catholics, Protestants, Jews, Muslims and Buddhists. Some of them still attended traditional religious institutions, but were so inspired by their contact with the Rathbuns that they eagerly sought participation in their groups.

Because of the diversity in these groups, I learned a great deal about other religions. I found that the "Golden Rule" was included in nearly all formal religious scriptures:

> Buddhism: "Hurt not others in ways that you yourself would find hurtful." Udanavarga 5:18

> Hinduism: "Do naught unto others which would cause you pain if done to you." Mahabharata 5:1517

> Judaism: "What is hateful to you; do not to your fellow man." Talmud, Chabbat 31a

> Islam: "No one of you is a believer until he desires for his brother that which he desires for himself." Sunan

> Christianity: "All things whatsoever you would that men should do to you, do ye even so to them." Matthew 7:12

> Confucianism: "Do not unto others what you would not have them do unto you." Analects 15:23

I felt I had been thrown a life preserver. With well-trained leaders, we argued, questioned and compared, sharing our individual life challenges. We found that Sharman's new approach to old scriptures presented rational solutions to real life problems. Over and over, the familiar scriptures of my childhood were clarified as having answers to the predicament in which I now found myself. I had never liked the scripture that stated, "It is better to give than to receive." I felt trapped in my present life situation where the demands seemed out of balance. I was giving everything I could and receiving very little. Doctors tried to prepare me for this imbalance when they came from the twelve hour surgery and told me: "You will be totally responsible for your husband from now on." My new understanding of scripture made clear that it was not <u>possible</u> to give without receiving and that the law of cause and effect insured that none of my giving was in vain. "You cast your bread upon the waters," it comes back to you, you know not where (Ecclesiastes, Chapter 11). This let me drop my resentment and trust the laws of cause and effect. More contemporary teachers such as Victor Frankel, Carl Jung, Teilhard De Chardin and Christopher Isherwood were included in the study.

I studied and assumed leadership roles with this group for fourteen years, broadening my reading and study to include all forms of theology, psychology and literature. The people studying with the Rathbuns began to consider themselves a community in which my children were included in the family and camp activities. One weekend, two years after his lobotomy, Jack attended a seminar with me under their leadership. The compassion and understanding this community showed toward his severely damaged brain condition and unpredictable behavior made me feel included and protected. Surprisingly, the haven of safety in which I found myself was using the same scriptures I had studied in childhood but those scriptures now demonstrated a very loving manner of dealing with good and evil that I had never understood. I was no longer alone in my experience. In this setting I did not feel the object of pity. I began to resolve my anger and bitterness toward religious teachings that had confused and betrayed me. I began to form a new and reliable understanding of how the universe functions. Gradually, I applied these understandings to the environment of my daily life. Instead of seeking magic which according to organized religion could only be gained from worship, prayer and church membership, I found a reality in the laws of cause and effect that were an absolute and dependable function of creation.

At no time in the months of struggling to survive my husband's lobotomy had it been suggested that I could CHOOSE my response to this tragedy. Without understanding why, I had distanced myself from the hand-wringing, pitying friends who wanted to sympathize and support me in my dilemma. Gradually I became aware of how being the object of pity diminished me.

My desperate need for some relief from my real life suffering made me rapidly apply the truths I found in my discussion groups. A new definition of evil as: **anything that blocks the flow of life,** made "Resist not evil" my daily mantra. It soon became clear that by dropping my angry resistance to my husband's condition, I not only relaxed my body but freed positive energy which filled me with a sense of peace. By changing my previous script of "this is not fair—it is a grotesque mistake to remove a person's brain" to "<u>he</u> is not suffering and needs only our love," and "I am being given the opportunity to grow and learn in a very profound way," I found calm in the midst of storm.

In my professional work, it is now clear that this approach is the popular cognitive/behavioral model of therapy. Helping clients to recognize their power to change negative thinking to hopeful, energizing, and creative views of what life has dealt them continues to inspire me daily. Much of our thinking has been imposed in childhood, and is reinforced, as we continue life, by others who have been taught to see themselves and the world in the same way. I see clearly that my parents' historical period, which included WWI, the Depression and the struggle to regain stability that followed, had deeply affected the rules and admonitions I carried in my head. "Don't expect anything good and then you won't be disappointed." "If everything seems to be going well, get ready for the fall." "Don't ever discuss sex, religion or politics." "You cannot trust most people."

If these negative admonitions had remained unexamined by the adult I had become, my belief system would have remained paralyzed by a negative view of life. When I was able to change those admonitions to "the choice is <u>always</u> mine as to how I respond to life's challenges," I was free to choose a positive response. Upon examination and practice I found that the laws of cause and effect are dependable and operate twenty-four hours a day. For example, if anger is the response, both physical and emotional well being are blocked. This is law and not a choice.

So in the interest of physical and emotional health, anger must be processed and not held on to. Scripts for freeing ourselves from paralysis can replace old scripts of defeat. We need positive goals and choosing action steps to achieve them. Taking this action is a guarantee for positive outcome. (See Appendix C) If we face failure, we must examine the lessons learned and re-set the goals. We must be willing to accept people as they are, not as we want them to be, and communicate about everything but not while in a negative emotional state. First we must claim the emotions as our own and process them appropriately.

It turned out that the simple act of withdrawing resistance to something that has already happened was my answer. In order to do this I needed to surrender my will to the reality in front of me and carefully monitor my thoughts, watching for old, negative phrases that would sabotage my goal of acceptance and positive action. In this way, I was able to direct all of my energy toward a creative, or life producing consequence. I saw the positive effect of surrender, something which I had seen as weak and ineffectual.

As I began to withdraw blame from doctors, hospitals and God, I experienced a flood of power and became an active participant in creating what I wanted as the outcome of my life challenges. I accepted "Diamonds are formed through heat and pressure," and believed that for me and our three children the outcome of this tragedy would be made positive in the end. In dropping my refusal to accept my husband's condition, I found myself able to stop wishing for his death. I was able to love him without reservation and most surprisingly, my change in attitude seemed to give him a sense of safety and peace that was obvious to the whole family and to his doctors.

BACK AT THE OFFICE

Far more often than I was taught to expect in graduate school, religion and spiritual beliefs become a part of psychotherapy. This happens when using psychodynamics, behavioral, cognitive or Rogerian approaches. Carl Jung, a leading theoretician, put an emphasis on psychological and spiritual dynamics that helped me bring the two together during my studies with the Rathbuns. When following the thought of a client in a therapy session, I have offered possible ways in which to resolve their confusion and pain. Many times they have responded with their own question: "Where did you learn that?"

It is only then that I share my own successful search to resolve the pain from life's challenges. There have been so many, many cases in my office when the experiences of immediate challenges and religious teachings have conflicted and contributed to a state of depression, or at the least an angry rejection of traditional beliefs. The frequency of these issues surfacing in the therapeutic setting makes it impossible to report only one definitive case. More often than not, a new understanding of historical religious writings has allowed clients to put their destructive self-judgment aside. I will, therefore, rather than report on one clinical case, outline my general knowledge and present beliefs regarding Christianity, the religion to which I was born, knowing that these same truths are present in most religions.

What I discovered was that Jesus was the best psychologist I could possibly have as a teacher. Putting aside doctrine, dogma, canon, or organized institutional rules, his teachings as a Jewish citizen in Israel when it was occupied by the Romans were revealed to be a most thorough examination of the rules of cause and effect which remain in place today. Knowledge of the laws of Creation which include physical, mental, emotional and spiritual life as taught by this incredibly insightful teacher can make sense of the most painful human conditions and present tools for survival, all of which are within reach.

One of the most important documents in these teachings was "The Sermon on The Mount." Understanding the historical period in which Jesus presented the concepts in this sermon shed new light to me on his mission and dedication. He saw the dilemma of his fellow Jews struggling under Roman rule and clearly saw their mistakes in dealing with the invaders. He saw that his people did not see the inevitable consequences of the events taking place when they were returning hatred for hatred, violence for violence and claiming that all problems were external, rather than internal.

He began to speak out. His insights, inspiration, genius, and clarity were so profound that crowds began to gather and listen wherever he went. It soon became evident to the Romans that this man threatened their power in Israel, and Jesus immediately recognized that he was a "person of interest" when Roman troops began to keep watch over him.

It became his strategy to move from place to place with his teachings, leaving his students with the admonition, "Let those who have ears to hear, hear, and those who have eyes to see, see." He could not linger to argue or reinforce his lessons lest the many schemes being carried out to arrest him succeed. His model of disclaiming responsibility for what others hear has given me the freedom to let go of expectations with clients as to what they are ready to hear or how fast they are able to change behavior and act on new perceptions. Acknowledging my limited power has allowed me to be content with the opportunity to plant seeds which grow and flower in their own time, not mine. (Parable of the mustard seed, Matt 13:31) It has given me patience in accepting my own halting growth. Knowing that the inevitability of outcome is ruled by the law of cause and effect gives meaning to the word "faith." I have complete faith in outcome, knowing that when the right conditions have been fulfilled, the outcome will reflect those conditions.

When it was evident he would be captured, Jesus carefully planned that event by going to Jerusalem, the stronghold of the Romans, where he would have the greatest audience for his final lesson at the time of Passover. Although his teaching had always been that our spiritual, or natural, body was our highest relationship to God or Creation, he knew that few believed him and in giving up his physical body, he would demonstrate the truth of his message through personal sacrifice.

He sent out word that he would give a lecture, or summarize his lessons in a final sermon. When the time arrived and he looked about at those who had come to listen, he saw only "the suffering." He had publicized the presentation of his sermon for some time and saw that none of the intellectuals or professionals had come. He found himself speaking only to those who were in pain for one reason or another, and so he began by pointing out that we are usually blessed with insight and learning when we suffer—not because suffering is necessary, but because it is so often the way humans learn. For most of us, it is only when our lives are shattered that we are ready to re-evaluate our strongly held beliefs. Even though it is painful, we seek refuge in old familiar scripts.

He began his sermon by reassuring his fellow Jews that he was not destroying their beliefs, but was clarifying an important fact regarding the source of behavior. He pointed out that all behavior begins with an emotional state. Actually, he was about to tell them that they were following the wrong path, but he used his beginning statement as a strategy to keep their minds open and to keep them from feeling attacked. This opening statement has been known as "The Beatitudes."

Acknowledging that he was speaking to the poor, the hungry, the sorrowful, and the persecuted, Jesus launched into correcting the belief that the source of human pain comes from outside us or in the action we take when we feel compelled by an outer stimulant. We like to say, "She made me do it," or "He gives me a pain." "No," Jesus said, "Our actions come from an inner feeling." We have the power to choose our response. When we blame an outer cause, we accept the role of victim and respond to it accordingly. A current way of stating Jesus' concept is that "all victims are volunteers."

In his ground-breaking sermon, Jesus went on to explain that stealing comes from greed, adultery comes from lust, and killing comes from anger. He pointed out that all of those sins listed in the Ten Commandments come from inner feelings which motivate the behavior. Although the outside force may provoke the emotion inside us, it is still our emotion and the same force can provoke a different emotion in another person. It is in confronting those inner feelings, or addressing the psychology of the event that gives us a choice as to how we respond to the outer force. In approaching our inner turmoil in this fashion, we can find the solution to changing behavior so that it favors life instead of destruction, or good instead of evil. He further explained that resisting those negative feelings without dealing with them, or "resisting evil", keeps that person from being "at one" (needing at-onement or atonement) with the flow of life.

In psychology I have found the major task for helping clients is to empower them to listen to their inner voice and to decide against blocking life, either their own or others. What is called the Devil in biblical scriptures has been called our "shadow side" by theorist Carl Jung. Jesus illustrated with his own behavior how he had to struggle against this darker side of his humanity. When he discovered the power of his teachings and found himself gathering huge audiences both inside and outside the temples, he struggled with how to use this power. He saw that he could become a king, or a general, or at the least, a great and famous hero. After his struggle with more egoistic roles, Jesus decided that the best way to use his power was to teach. His example of carefully considering these alternatives by spending forty days and forty nights in a state of contemplation could well be followed by world leaders when they are faced with struggles with their own ego state.

One of the most often-faced tasks of a psychotherapist is to help other human beings deal with their anger. Jesus' way of putting this was to say, "When you would come to the altar and have anger with your brother, go first and make peace with your brother." In all of his teachings, his reference to "coming to the altar," implied your arrival at inner peace and harmony. It was never his instruction that you should never have anger or that if you did experience anger, you were a bad person. He simply stated the truth of cause and effect – that you cannot experience the calm and flow of a full life when you are in a state of anger. He recommended that you acknowledge and resolve your anger.

His passion for saving his people from certain destruction led him to gather help in the form of disciples and to move swiftly from one location to another, thus making it hard for the Romans to silence him. How much better off many people who come to my office would be if they could follow Jesus' example. Many people spend their lives wishing others to be different …to change in a way that would be more acceptable to them. They continually pour out criticism and spend hours lamenting the flaws in their parents or in their spouse while feeling drained of their life energy. How much more life-giving it would be if they could accept those they resist as they are and move on to health and well-being on their own soul journey. Jesus refused to condemn those who were judged by the mobs. By his accepting them as they were he stimulated changes in their behavior and health that were claimed to be "miracles" by the crowds who observed them.

In many instances when he was credited with performing miracles, Jesus disclaimed that credit and declared "your faith has made you whole." The most powerful teacher also models their teachings.

Many of Jesus' teachings can only be understood when seen as symbolic or mythical. His style of teaching was dramatic and moving. "If your hand offendeth thee, cut if off. If your eye offendeth thee, pluck it out." Thus, he repeatedly put the responsibility for offense directly on the shoulders of the actor. There is no help for any emotional state as long as blame is placed on external forces. Blame is a declaration of helplessness, and this was continually rejected as a way to proceed.

There is no question that Jesus' style of teaching and demonstration through his own behaviors caught the attention of his listeners. In his genius he told stories (parables) in which only those who were beginning to understand could see the lesson. Those bent upon stopping him, not understanding the hidden truth in the stories, had no proof that he was a troublemaker. When confronted by their determination to stop him, he charmingly capitulated stating, "When in Rome, do as the Romans do," at the same time warning his followers not to rebel when they were overpowered.

When the inevitability of his crucifixion came to pass, even as he suffered physical pain, Jesus used this tragedy to teach one last lesson to Mary whom he saw weeping and wailing at the foot of his cross. "Mary, Mary, look beside you," he told her "the man beside you is your son." Thus did he point out the necessity of directing our caring and nurturing to those who live rather than staying at the grave to weep. And thus did he point out that we need not limit our loving attentions to our biological family, but must extend them to whomever we find beside us.

More often than I can relate here, these psychological teachings and the genius behind them have been key in helping clients become empowered to make inner changes that heal and change their pain to life-giving energy.

AFTERWORD

LESSONS LEARNED

There have been many surprises as I've journeyed through life. Many of them were jarring and unwelcome while some were heartwarming and delightful. Whether positive or negative they have all provided insights and enlightenment that I am attempting to share with others by writing this book and through my professional work with clients. In doing so

I have discovered the great privilege of experiencing intimate thoughts and feelings with other individuals and the fact that we each have our story of success, failure and growth. Through my work with clients I have had many personal life lessons confirmed over and over again. This confirmation does not provide proof which can be accepted as scientific data. There is a formula that must be followed in order to claim scientific truth. That formula claims that a hypothesis must be proven by being predictable, measurable and repeatable.

When it comes to proving facts regarding human emotions and the behavior that follows those feelings, the variables make it extremely difficult. The scientific formula for truth does not allow for conditioned concepts of life, since individuals are frequently unaware of their conditioned script. Another variable includes the factor of mind changing and developmental stages which can be arrested or hastened. When the criteria of this formula are not met, the scientific world calls it simply, "anecdotal evidence." There may be a time when the criteria for scientific data can be met when dealing with emotional factors but in the meantime scientific proof does not seem necessary as we observe similar behaviors among humans all over the planet and work to understand the implications of our growing consciousness. It seems our lessons are not finished as long as we live, so it is with this understanding that I will attempt to summarize some of those lessons which have been most helpful in my ongoing role as a student of life.

States of Consciousness

It was helpful for me, in my ongoing search for truth, to learn that we all have three states of consciousness: the conscious mind, the subconscious mind and the unconscious mind. The conscious mind is full of rules and concepts that we have learned in our life experience. It is as though we all carry a very big library in our conscious mind and most of our daily interactions with the outside world are governed by the books in that library. These books contain rules learned in childhood, as well as conclusions from challenges and victories experienced up to the present time.

When many of my childhood rules and experiences began to conflict with my adult experiences, I was forced to choose which books in that library I needed to discard. This can be an unsettling experience because discarding strongly held beliefs will leave a period of uncertainty, where there had been certainty. My childhood belief that goodness would lead to safety had to be discarded in order to avoid a growing rage as my losses increased, and to accept that there was richness in learning the lessons of life as an adult. I was forced to question each and every source of authority that I had accepted as a child and to measure truth by new criteria. All of this was done with a conscious need to understand life as it was unfolding, not as I wished it to be. It required self awareness as to what went on in the conscious mind that was controlled by earlier conclusions I was only mildly aware of.

The subconscious mind contains our private observations and ruminations concerning ourselves and the outside world and serves as a channel between the conscious and unconscious minds when we sleep. We are usually aware of the travels of the subconscious through self talk, dreams, or intuitions and make choices as to whether to reveal material existing there to the outside world. Many folks have been taught to ignore the activity in the subconscious or it has been devalued as "silly" when expressed.

The unconscious mind is magically connected to what Carl Jung called a "universal wisdom" and contains both personal and global consciousness. Access to this level of understanding requires stilling the conscious mind and allowing the contents stored in the unconscious to be communicated symbolically in the form of dreams or intuitions. Many of us are unable to still the conscious mind and can only access this level when asleep. This difficulty makes it even more important that we pay attention to our sleeping dream life. Because this level of our mind communicates through pictures and feelings, it is sometimes very difficult to interpret the messages coming from that source. Additionally, since the contents of the unconscious mind have often been deliberately rejected in our conscious state because they are too traumatic, we would rather leave them there than have to process their meaning. When we deliberately keep them unconscious, we only add to their power and we can be driven and controlled by their power without knowing it. However, it is important to know that this level of our mind is always working in our favor and therefore it is important to pay attention to re-occurring dreams and feelings. The importance of the message coming from the unconscious can be measured by the intensity of feelings both during and when awakened from the dream.

Sometimes, in working with clients, it is only when they are able to communicate what is going on in their dream life that new information leads to healing. Information coming from the unconscious is never a form of prophecy or about other people. It is all about the dreamer and their present need to have insight into what is stored there. Material stored in the unconscious can have extraordinary power in our daily lives without our being aware of where the power is coming from. Although investigating this area of our mind used to take years in the form of psychoanalysis, there are contemporary methods which can help unravel the mysteries of the unconscious through brief therapy.

There are many theories regarding dream interpretation, but it was through understanding my dreams with Gestalt interpretation that I was finally able to face the deep, residual rage I carried from various challenges in life and to free myself from that burden. This great power in the unconscious mind can push us into irrational behavior that we find difficult to explain to ourselves or to others. The true function of the unconscious is to call attention to the fact that we are carrying unneeded baggage from the past, or to have experiences in dreams that are not possible in our conscious state. Reunion with lost relationships or the experiences of flying are familiar to many of us. Painful though it might be, careful attention to material from the unconscious, whether it consists of nightmares or wish fulfillment dreams, is part of our responsibility to ourselves. The feelings and experiences in our dreams can be as satisfying as a conscious experience, or as terrifying as a horror movie, but they are calling for our attention.

Because of the pain I was experiencing in my life, I seemed to draw people to myself who helped me understand the power of the unconscious and to draw on its help in understanding my own reactions. Once I learned that the unconscious was always trying to help me, and was not focused on prophecy or another person's destiny, I paid close attention to understanding my conditioned view of life. Carl Jung made an incredible contribution to our understanding when he recognized that our job was to bring the conscious and unconscious minds together in self awareness in order to make creative choices in response to our daily lives. His concept of "universal wisdom," which he claims is available to everyone, made a huge difference in my ability to claim insights and ideas without needing to document their source.

Expression of Feelings

Nearly all of the complexities of our inner life have to do with our indifference to feelings. There are three ways we deal with feelings and only one of them results in a healthy emotional life. We can REpress our feelings, or successfully ignore their existence and thus assign them to the unconscious. We can SUPpress our feelings thus keeping them to ourselves even though we know they exist, or we can EXpress our feelings in some appropriate manner. Only the EXpression of feelings, especially those negative feelings that constrict the body processes, deals with them in a healthy way. If feelings are not expressed, DEpression often results.

Although in the 60's and 70's we were encouraged to go to those whom we believed caused our feelings and tell them how they made us feel, we know now that those feelings belong only to us. To hold on to blame requires that you accept the identity of victim. No matter what has occurred, accepting that you have chosen your response empowers you to remain in charge of your ongoing life. If you give this power to an outside source you are declaring impotency. In reality, all victims are volunteers.

When negative feelings are expressed as blame or attack toward another person, it is nearly always destructive. Writing, screaming (in private), punching a punching bag, throwing a bowling ball and naming the pins, crying, hugging, smiling, laughing or exercise are all ways of expressing feelings appropriately. If our feeling is strong and we are unable to articulate its source we can still begin the EXpression, rational or not. This sometimes leads to an unveiling of the source of the feeling. Other times, it is such a relief to release the constrictive energy that we are able to move on in our growth without losing the energy required to repress feelings.

Because the period of history in which I was raised negated feelings and demanded that they be suppressed, it took some time for me to be able to face my true feelings. Learning to share unwanted feelings with another who could accept them without judgment was a task that took even longer to complete, but having at least one person who can listen with detachment is essential. Sometimes there can be a period of life where only a professional can fill this neutral role in helping us express our feelings. However, to keep them in the body can result in additional stress from illness. Depression of emotions also depresses our immune system.

Self Empowerment

There are many times in our lives when we feel utterly impotent and without any power to change our circumstances. At such times it is difficult to find an appropriate action and it is easy to fall into depression or victimization.

It was such a time when I faced Jack's condition after the lobotomy. If I looked at the mountain of depressing circumstances – the effect on the children – the loss of his support for me – the problem of meeting our financial needs – the confusion of family and friends who did not know all of the facts about his condition, and the tragic fact that his life as a normal man was no longer a possibility, I was frozen in a sense of hopelessness and unable to act. It was not until I became aware that I was looking up at a mountain of despair instead of staying with the moment, that I felt any possibility of surviving the effect of such a colossal pinnacle of negativity. It was through the guidance of teachers and friends that I decided I must put one foot in front of the other, keeping my eyes only on the next step and not on the mountain before me. In doing this I felt some relief, but mostly I felt empowered to take that next step. It was not until I refocused on the present moment instead of the mountain that I had the energy to be fully alive and meet the challenges we all faced.

As a therapist, I have found it important to help clients see that this involves a choice. It involves the choice to stop the defeating thoughts, clear the mind and be present. This approach has been fully explored in more recent times by a method called "mindfulness." In working with clients, I have created a metaphor for helping individuals see that no matter what the circumstances, we still have a choice as to our response to life's challenges. This choice does not involve changing the circumstances, but claims power in choosing our response. In other words, pain is a given, but ongoing suffering is a choice. A creative choice is usually only apparent after the feelings have been faced and some form of physical process has taken place such as crying, shouting, hitting appropriate objects or having a sympathetic ear to which the feelings can be expressed.

The metaphor for going down the road of life which has been most helpful to me is to see ourselves as a vehicle in which our three ego states (the child, the adult and the parent ego states) ride together. The key factor for a successful journey is dependent upon which of those ego states is in the driver's seat. Just as we choose our speed and destination when driving a car, we must accept that we choose how we are going to feel by the thoughts we have in response to what is happening in our lives. Three different ego states will have three different views of the same circumstances when making life decisions. If we allow the "child" to be in the driver's seat, our choices will be dominated by our childish script of blame or victimization. In most cases, except when a child's spontaneity and adventure are the goal, we must keep the "adult" in the driver's seat so that all our wisdom acquired at that point in life can be applied. Having the "parent" ego state in the front passenger seat can be a help and comfort when tense situations arise, but the "child" should be in the back seat in restraints until we have time to play. The parent state is the one which comforts us, suggests ways to get help and accepts us just as we are. Learning to use that state to re-parent ourselves when our parenting has been inadequate takes time and focus and sometimes a model outside ourselves to show us how.

Many of us were taught to "trust" our feelings – that they were a gauge for truth. Now we know through studies in biofeedback, relaxation, imagery, and meditation that our feelings are determined by our thoughts. In facing our feelings we must also face the thoughts which create them and from what authority those thoughts have originated. When considering a negative thought, the most important question we must ask ourselves is "who says?"

In continuing down the highway of life, imagine how your journey would go if the highway signs on the freeway were "Despair, next Right" or "Fear, ¼ mile" or "Hope, ½ mile" or "Inner Peace, 200 miles". Why would we choose to take the next off ramp towards Despair when we could stay on the road and find Inner Peace? In order to make a positive choice about the direction we choose, we must know what thoughts are racing through our mind. We must be aware of our thoughts at all times, knowing that they will cause feelings and that feelings have a biological effect as well as determining our behavior. Why would we choose to cause ourselves to age much faster by increasing our heart rate, keeping our muscles tense, flooding our digestive system with unneeded acids, and cutting our oxygen supply by hyperventilating. There can be times when we leave the freeway for a short period to refuel and rest from the pressures in our life. These refueling periods can be organized retreats, vacations, or simply staying in bed for a day. They can also be periods of introspection which bring self awareness. This is the first step toward being in charge of your life.

Many people have been misled by exaggerated claims about positive thinking. There is a process by which we can arrive at a healthy, positive approach to challenge but it includes acknowledging the feelings that surge through our body and which were not determined by our choice. When these painful, unwanted feelings arrive, we must acknowledge them and, if necessary, express them in some way that relieves the body. It is only then that we can choose to replace negative thinking by finding hopeful, creative thoughts. There is no such thing as "false hope". The two words are incongruent. And our thinking need never rule out "miracles." Miracles are simply happenings that we do not yet understand. We cannot shortcut the change to positive thinking by simply declaring that it is what we will do.

Perhaps this is best illustrated by the Psalms. Most of us were taught the comfort of the 23rd Psalm which includes, "Yea, though I walk through the valley of the shadow of death, I will fear no evil for thou art with me." To arrive at this place of peace and comfort is a natural desire. But the 22nd Psalm has been ignored. This Psalm clearly illustrates the process by which we find ourselves empowered to enjoy that comfort in the following expression of feelings: "My God, my God, why hast thou forsaken me? Why art thou so far from helping me, and from the words of my roaring?" After releasing this expression of fear and anger, we can return to directing our thoughts to solutions without stressing our body and weighing down our heart. Clients have been surprised after declaring that they will heal their illness by thinking positively when I suggest that they might first need to have a tantrum or spend a few moments in self pity.

The Importance of Relationship

One of the most difficult aspects of life revolves around the fact that we are social organisms. We need to be in relationship with others. When young babies are not held, touched, or spoken to, they do not develop normally. When we are isolated, rejected or deprived of nurturance from others, we shut down our spectrum of feelings in order to protect ourselves from pain and sometimes become reclusive or violent.

For many whose value system sets material possessions and wealth at the top of their priorities, it comes as a major surprise to find that what they value most as they face their mortality is relationship. What most of us would like to have written in our obituary is, "She died surrounded by family and loved ones." Yet too often we lead lives dominated by our ignorance and lack of skill in carrying on healthy relationships. Learning to love unconditionally is promoted by most religions, but is a seemingly unattainable goal. When a healthy, wealthy, successful client sits down with a heavy sigh asking "Is this all there is?" it is clear that their value system has not been headed by the goal of healthy relationships. Interpersonal activities at every level provide unending challenge and reward to our ongoing lives, with the possibility of providing more satisfaction in rewards than any other pursuit.

One area of ignorance is the fact that men and women are wired differently. Carl Jung expertly differentiates between the opposites in his explanation of the masculine and feminine principles. Various periods of history have played out the balance of power between the sexes as right and wrong, when in truth, the two principles are complementary. In our more primitive eras of development, this complementariness was obvious. The masculine principle left the nest to kill the bears while the feminine principle bore the babies and tended to food.

At this point in history, the masculine/feminine principles can exist in either biological sex. However, they usually exist in both sexes in various states of development. We seem to be magnetized toward a person whose balance is complementary to our own and thus they represent some latent aspect of our development. Being by this other person's side creates a sense of wholeness. Regardless of our biological sex, what we seem to seek in relationship is a partner who will witness and validate our life. We need someone who promises to care about everything that goes on in our life, whether good or bad. **This does not mean enmeshment or dependency**. But if and when we face an overwhelming challenge, we know that person will be there for us. Then, believing that we have found such a person, we need to learn the skill of healthy communication. Love can only grow stronger when partners know on a daily basis how their behavior, their words, and their affections are experienced by their partner. We need to learn to say "Because I love you, I need to communicate my observations and my experiences in living by your side."

It is also important to accept that we may have periods of time in our lives when we are without a partner. Developing our inner center becomes our lifeline to avoid loneliness – to learn the value of solitude. We immediately know when we have been "knocked off our center" and can use the experience for further growth.

The very best unions are those when partners are not dependent on each other but have formed a relationship so authentic that they are open to each other in every way. To look at your partner and know that you are understood – that you are validated – that you are cared for – all of the time, every day, is the blessing of commitment. To know that our life does not go unnoticed and to know that both of our lives are enlarged and inspired when we look into the eyes of that loved one and know that we are "seen" is the gift we find in relationship.

Friendships bring many of the same gifts, but we sometimes have myths regarding friendships. Old friends are not necessarily the best friends. Certainly it is satisfying to have shared part of our history with that old friend and therefore to have memories worth discussing. But if we are growing and pursuing our own "soul journey" we often speed ahead or tag after someone with whom we have traveled for a period of time. It is very acceptable to notice and to admit that you no longer have common interests with an old friend. Your journeys can often take you in different directions. When we stop in the comfort of old friendships we can sometimes stagnate our growth in consciousness. I have retained friendships from high school and when or if we meet, it is as if we never parted. But the bulk of our life is more focused on our present journey and we may have taken different paths in our religious, political and family activities and are now more bonded with friends who share our direction

Looking Forward – The Importance of Goals

Knowing why you get out of bed in the morning and looking forward to another day of life is a certain formula for continuing health and well being. This is true whether you are a cancer patient, in a state of grief, or leading a happy, healthy life. However, for too many of us, a goal has become an obligation and we are following old rules which mandate that we must finish what we start. No, we don't! If goals come from our own inner desires and are not imposed by external authorities, we can drop them, change them, or continue to work toward them at our own pace. Having workable goals inspires and energizes us.

When we reach the finish line of life, it is important to have no regrets, no unfinished business, and a willingness to depart from our physical body. Since we don't know when the finish line may appear, this exhorts us to live each day openly and fully as Elisabeth Kubler-Ross suggests in my opening quote. My belief system includes my owning a spiritual body that can continue in whatever level of existence there may be. To feel gratitude for the life I have lived and love for those who accompanied me is a great reward I take with me.

APPENDIX A

RULES OF COMMUNICATION

FOR CONFLICT

"Give sorrow words. The grief that does not speak whispers the oer-fraught heart and bids it break."

-Shakespeare

I. BRING IT UP!! SOON!!

The longer you let it simmer, the more energy you give it.

II. BE CIVILIZED—KEEP COOL—FLIGHT FAIR

It's no longer cool to throw things or holler. This only adds to an already heated situation. It may feel good -- that's why children do it. Talk it out.

III. DON'T TELL EACH OTHER WHAT TO DO.

Use I statements, not you statements. Express feelings as well as facts. Tell the other person about your experience — not about your mental judgment.

IV. BE SURE EACH HAS THEIR SAY BEFORE YOU PART.

Even if there is no solution in sight, be sure everything gets said. Ask "what else?" and listen.

(continued)

APPENDIX A (continued)

V. <u>STICK TO THE SUBJECT.</u>

If you keep wandering off the subject at hand, you need to set another time to deal with the other subject. No repetitious issues from past history. Keep a list of things you would like to talk about. Choose a time and place where there will be no interruptions.

VI. <u>IF THERE IS NO SOLUTION IN SIGHT.</u>

Be willing to put it on the back burner and come back to it another time. Set the new time before you part.

(continued)

10-12 MINUTE REFLECTIVE LISTENING EXERCISE
HOT BUTTON ISSUES

(To be used when it's difficult to be rational. If necessary, a timer can be set.)

I. First, the two communicators agree on time limits for speaking, usually two or three minutes. The speaker tells the listener what is on their mind. The listener may not interrupt, argue, deny, question, or add to the recitation.

The listener now tells the speaker what they heard beginning with "I heard you say ————————." They must include everything that was said and reflect it back correctly. The speaker may correct the listener or point out deletions.

Now repeat the above, reversing the speaker and listener until all has been said.

II. When finished, each communicator asks themselves the following questions:

Did I learn anything new?
Does it change my perspective?
Do I see solutions?
Was I completely honest?
Can I accept that we see things differently—not right
    or wrong, but differently?

General discussion on these questions can follow, but it is also okay to leave the discussion if it becomes tiring and come back at a later time to repeat the exercise. It may take several times of repeating this exercise before the topic is resolved. That's okay. It's in process!!

APPENDIX B

FEELINGS AS GUIDE

Our body is a very reliable instrument for giving us messages about ourselves. The body is not interested in what is going on outside of us, but is working 100% of the time for our, and only our, well being. What is perceived visually or audibly is registered in the central nervous system, but not always interpreted correctly there. Our central nervous system is headed by the brain and contains all the rules, regulations, attitudes, self image, beliefs, and decisions which we have gathered in our lifetime of learning to survive. Therefore, we cannot always trust our mind to give us an unbiased and objective message about what is going on. Our mind is busy sifting through years of information and looking for an interpretation or perception that fits our belief system. However, our bodies do not pay attention to our conditioned mind. Our body simply responds. Therefore, our body is respons-able and can guide us in being aware of reactions that have not yet been processed or have been incorrectly processed in our mental network.

Too often we have been taught to give others the responsibility for our feelings. "They hurt my feelings." "He made me angry." "She drives me crazy." In reality, no one else "causes" our feelings. Someone else's behavior evokes a feeling response in us, but the feelings are ours and are a very important message to us about *our own behavior.*

(continued)

FEELING	MESSAGE
ANGER	Something is not going the way I want it to.
RESENTMENT	I am doing something I should not be doing, or I must change the attitude with which I am doing it.
FEAR	I am facing some kind of danger—physical mental, emotional, or spiritual.
GUILT	I am now or have in the past violated my own standards or accepted someone else's.
ANXIETY	I am caught in the past or the future. I am not fully present.
LOVE	I am in a state of connectedness with someone or something else.
GRATITUDE	I have been validated by someone, or something outside myself.
DEPRESSION	Feelings are sunken in. DEpressed, not EXpressed.

When we find that we experience negative feelings, we can address a change by starting from either end of the cycle. We can listen to the message in the feelings and change our thoughts and behavior, or we can change our behavior and evoke different feelings.

THE CHOICE IS OURS

APPENDIX C

OPTIONS FOR ACTION

<u>EXPRESS IT</u> Talk, cry, shout. To a friend, family member, counselor, priest, minister, neighbor, or the wall. Writing, singing, dancing, or striking appropriate objects are also helpful forms of ex-pression.

<u>RELAXATION AND IMAGERY</u> Alone or with others, relax the body using whatever technique works best for you. Then, while in a relaxed state, focus your mind on positive images which heal, reframe, or bring strength. Many tapes are available as aids for this exercise. Get a massage to familiarize yourself with how the body feels when relaxed—then practice returning to that state by using deep breathing and your mind.

<u>EXERCISE</u> Any body movement that is appropriate for you can help break up depression and anxiety. Add aesthetic surroundings or music to feel more "yourself." The more totally you are involved in body movement, the more release you will feel from the stressor.

<u>LOOK FOR MEANING AND VALUE</u> In-spirit yourself by searching for understanding and growth when challenged by a painful life event. Resources for this include your religion, books, self-help education and support groups, friends and family. Inspiration comes when it is sought.

Professional therapists can assist you in discovering what it is you may have forgotten about yourself and provide a neutral field upon which to project your confusion. Allow yourself some support.

(continued)

<u>SET GOALS AND ACTION STEPS</u> Take control of your life by planning for tomorrow. One day at a time—know what you want tomorrow and act on that knowledge today.

A single moment can retroactively flood an entire life with meaning.

Victor Frankl –"The Doctor and the Soul"

BIBLIOGRAPHY

This is a partial list of those books which have meant
the most to me as a student and as a teacher.

Benson,M.D., Herbert, THE RELAXATION RESPONSE, Harper Torch, 1975 THE MIND/BODY EFFECT, Simon & Schuster, 1970

Claremont de Castillejo, Irene, KNOWING WOMAN, Harper @ Row, 1973

Frankel, Victor, MAN'S SEARCH FOR MEANING, Washington Square Press, 1946

Fromm, Erick, THE FORGOTTEN LANGUAGE, Grove Press, Inc., 1951

Gibran, Kahlil, THE PROPHET, Alfred Knopf, 1964

Johnson, Robert A. HE, SHE, Religious Publishing Co. 1974

Jung, Carl, MAN AND HIS SYMBOLS, Dell, 1964

Kubler-Ross, Elisabeth, ON DEATH AND DYING, Simon and Schuster, 1969; DEATH, THE FINAL STAGE OF GROWTH, Prentice-Hall, 1975

Kunkel, Fritz, IN SEARCH OF MATURITY, Charles Scribner Sons, 1943

LeShan, Larry, CANCER AS A TURNING POINT, E.P. Dutton, 1989

(continued)

Missildine, W. Hugh, YOUR INNER CHILD OF THE PAST, Simon & Schuster, 1963

Ornish, Dean, STRESS, DIET AND YOUR HEART, Holt, Rinehart and Winston, 1982

Peck, M. Scott, THE ROAD LESS TRAVELED, Simon & Schuster, 1978

Rathbun, Harry, CREATIVE INITIATIVE, Creative Initiative Foundation, 1976

Rogers, Carl R., ON BECOMING A PERSON, Houghton Mifflin Co., 1961

Samuels, Mike and Nancy, SEEING WITH THE MIND'S EYE, Random House, 1975

Shrock, PhD, Dean, DOCTOR'S ORDERS: GO FISHING, First Publishers Group, Ltd., 2000

Simonton, O. Carl, GETTING WELL AGAIN, Bantam, 1978

Teilhard de Chardin, BUILDING THE EARTH, Dimension Books, 1965

CPSIA information can be obtained at www.ICGtesting.com
Printed in the USA
LVOW090339051011

249091LV00004B/1/P